Preaching Women

Preaching Women

Gender, Power and the Pulpit

Liz Shercliff

scm press

© Liz Shercliff 2019

Published in 2019 by SCM Press
Editorial office
3rd Floor, Invicta House,
108–114 Golden Lane,
London EC1Y 0TG, UK
www.scmpress.co.uk

SCM Press is an imprint of Hymns Ancient & Modern Ltd
(a registered charity)

Ancient
&Modern

Hymns Ancient & Modern® is a registered trademark of
Hymns Ancient & Modern Ltd
13A Hellesdon Park Road, Norwich,
Norfolk NR6 5DR, UK

Scripture quotations are from the New Revised Standard Version
of the Bible, Anglicized Edition, copyright © 1989, 1995 by the
Division of Christian Education of the National Council of the
Churches of Christ in the USA. Used by permission. All rights
reserved.

British Library Cataloguing in Publication data

A catalogue record for this book is available
from the British Library

978-0-334-05838-0

Typeset by Regent Typesetting

Contents

For all those who have challenged,
championed and chosen to journey with me,
particularly David Shercliff, Dan Shercliff
and Ruth Curry.

Thanks go particularly to Elizabeth Stokes,
who devoted much time to reading the
first draft.

Foreword
Women's Voices are God's Voice

In 2015, as Bishop of Stockport, I learned of plans for a new conference. Its aim was to encourage and equip women preachers. I admired and encouraged both the concept and the content, and the first 'Women's Voices' conference was held in June 2015. It followed the publication in *The Preacher* magazine of an article by Liz Shercliff: 'Do Women Preach with a Different "Voice"?' In exploring women's preaching, the conference considered in particular why and how women preachers might help speak the faith and life experiences of women, and women Christians in particular. The most common comments on that first event were: 'I thought it was only me' and 'Please could we have another conference?'

Since then Women's Voices has become an annual event in the Diocese of Chester, and is usually fully booked months in advance. It seeks to pioneer the development of women's preaching by combining practical homiletics with academic rigour. Important and transforming questions have been addressed: Why do we need to hear women's voices? How can we make safe spaces in Bible study and liturgy for all, including women? Can we read the Bible as women? What difference does it make if we do?

So I was delighted to be asked to introduce the fourth annual conference in 2018. The invitation prompted me to reflect on the importance of women's voices. Their importance in Scripture, the Church and the world. Their importance for women and men. Their importance in recognizing which voices are heard and which silenced; which voices used and which denied.

In my address at the conference, I shared a comment I have sometimes made: it was a surprise to me to discover, when I was announced as the next Bishop of Stockport in 2014, and the first 'woman bishop' in the Church of England, that I was a woman! Not that I have ever doubted that fact, or desired to be anything other than a woman.

Being ordained priest in 1994, I've had decades of my gender being commented on and reacted to (positively as well as negatively) in my exercise of ministry – but I really didn't think of myself as a 'woman' anything. I'm just me. Who happens to be a woman.

I've been and done many things in my life, and I've been blessed by sharing and living them alongside men as well as women. I've been child, sibling, friend, scholar, spouse, ordinand, deacon, parent, priest. I've spent time as curate, chaplain, trainer, team vicar, Director of Ordinands, incumbent, Dean for Women in Ministry, participant observer, and now bishop. Being the first woman to be named bishop meant it was my being a *woman* that attracted attention, so I've had to give my own attention to what that means for me as well as for others.

I have learned to recognize and give greater voice to the women in the Church who nurtured and influenced me: Janet and others, whose love and hospitality was a sacrament of God's love and helped bring me to faith; Liz Shercliff herself, who as one of my youth group leaders encouraged my gifts and gave me a safe space to test them; Mrs Marshall (even as an adult I can't quite bring myself to call her by her first name), whose own love of theology engendered that love in me; Helen, whose pioneering example, entirely unknown to her, inspired me to take seriously my vocation to ordination; Margaret, whose faith and nurture brought me to acceptance for ordination training; Sarah and Jan and others, who have accompanied me in striving for faithful obedience to that calling ... the list goes on and on.

I have learned to honour and name, even where their names are not recorded, the women in Scripture whose part in God's salvation history, though vital, is often untold or diminished. I have learned that in their story, God's story becomes my story, not just because I'm a woman but because we all need to listen to the whole story. I've learned to be more confident in refusing to collude with the false image of God as male because that not only diminishes me and all women, but much more importantly diminishes God. I am passionate about finding and listening to women in the Bible. If we don't, we risk closing our ears and hardening our hearts to the voice of God.

And I've learned that it matters to people, men and women, boys as well as girls, that a woman holds this space. That it gives hope, that it is good news, that it points to the Kingdom of God, a kingdom of freedom and forgiveness, of justice and peace, of holiness and grace. Not that I embody those things but that if even I can hold this place it means God offers those things. I'm learning to cherish this honour as a gift not for my sake but as a signpost to God's love for all. As others have been examples and inspirations for me, so I need to take seriously that I am that for countless others, outside as well as within the Church, of all faiths and none. I've discovered that I'm a named part of the national curriculum! – just one indicator of the considerable influence I hold, and for Christ's sake, I must not waste or discard it.

I remain convinced that it is vital for all of us, women and men, young and old, from our diverse heritages and circumstances, to 'find our own voice'. There is value in recognizing and valuing women's spirituality, and discerning where it overlaps and complements, supplements and enhances, confronts and challenges that of our brothers – so we all can be drawn closer to the Living God who is at work in us.

Following the 2018 Women's Voices I was asked to write an article for *The Preacher*[1] magazine, articulating some of what lay behind my short contribution to the conference – a lovely reflection of the journey that inspired Liz Shercliff to initiate Women's Voices in the first place. I wrote along these lines:

---

1 *The Preacher* 174: 2019.

'Thus says the Lord ... Listen to my voice, and do all that I command you. So you shall be my people, and I will be your God' (Jer. 11.3–4).

God's own voice is neither male nor female. But as we all, both male and female, are made in God's image, all our voices echo something of the voice of God. When women's voices are not heard, we are deaf, at least in part, to the word of God. And muting, at least in part, the voice of God.

We must therefore be attentive to the voices of women in Scripture. For example, as we read of the God of Abraham, the God of Isaac, the God of Jacob, we must also listen out for the voice of the God of Sarah, Hagar and Keturah, the God of Rebecca, the God of Leah and Rachel, and Bilhah and Zilpah. Salvation history is told through the stories of women as well as men. We have to listen harder to hear God through such women's voices; they have so often been muted. We have to listen even harder for those women who are unnamed and passed by, because so often what God is saying in and through them is drowned out by the louder noise of the men around them.

This work of hearing women's voices matters. When we do not listen to women, we are being deaf to the voice of God.

It is not only the narratives of Scripture that specifically include women that might help us listen to God more carefully and completely. God speaks, reaches out, loves, through every word of Scripture, *and God does not speak with a male voice*.

As I age, like most people, I am finding that my hearing diminishes. It is not only volume that makes a difference, there are pitches I find more difficult to hear. That means it takes more attention to follow some conversations; it is less likely that I can pick out particular sounds from cacophony; some music is harder to appreciate. If we only listen to particular or limited pitches of God's voice in Scripture, we are missing out – certainly, we are missing out on the fullness of all that God offers, and perhaps missing something significant and vital.

Both men and women need to listen out for God speaking with a woman's voice through all of Scripture if we are to hear God more clearly.

And further, it is not only in the words of Scripture itself that women's voices need to be heard. Women's voices are necessary as we respond and engage with Scripture. If women's voices are not heard in the study and proclamation of Scripture we risk losing for ourselves, or denying to others, the hope of salvation because we are listening only partially. As Thomas Cranmer taught us to pray:

> Blessed Lord, who caused all holy Scripture to be written for our learning, grant that we may in such wise hear, read, mark, learn and inwardly digest them, that by patience and comfort of thy holy Word, we may embrace and ever hold fast the blessed hope of eternal life.

All of Scripture is for each of us, and of each of us. None of us hears or understands completely, and we discover the truths of God together. What we are hearing and understanding will be warped and distorted, as well as limited if we ignore or marginalize the voices of women in our reception of Scripture.

When we do not hear what women hear, what women have read and marked and learned, if the ways that women have been nourished by the saving word of God are not recognized, we deny the work of God. When women's voices are silenced or disregarded, God is dishonoured, and, according to Cranmer's prayer, the promise of eternal life itself may slip from our grasp. Furthermore, when we ignore the damage done to women by poor exegesis, we discredit God.

When we do not listen to women, we are being deaf to the voice of God.

All this means, I think, that men and women alike (individually and together) need to be attentive and open, both to God's own voice sounding as a woman, and to the voices of women themselves that may be echoing the voice of God.

We women, therefore, need to take courage, and make our voices heard. If I do not speak, I am silencing something of God that cannot otherwise be spoken. We all have a responsibility to be attentive to the voice of God in women's voices. That may mean men taking responsibility not only not to drown us out, but to encourage our speaking. It also means women taking responsibility to use our own voices and amplify one another's voices.

For many of us that is hard. Centuries of conditioning have taught us to be silent, that we have nothing worth saying and that we won't be heard. Some of us prefer now to remain muted, and we do not want to hear that our voice is God's voice. That responsibility is too much.

My premise, though, is that we are denying God if we deny ourselves. It is ridiculous and outrageous – but it seems that God's voice is spoken and heard in and through fallen, fallible, fractured humanity, including women and girls – including me.

My voice is God's voice.

If it is true that when we do not listen to women, we are being deaf to the voice of God, it must also be true that when we women do not speak we are silencing the voice of God.

I think I have always known the truth in all this, though it has taken me years to recognize and articulate it. The prompt for this particular train of thought was being asked to introduce the Women's Voices conference. It provides an important opportunity for women and men to give attention to hearing God's voice in women, and for women to gain the confidence to speak up and speak out.

I do pray that God raises up more women to preach and teach and write and proclaim, in public places, the good news of Jesus Christ. Even though a few of us are now prominent in the Church and can make some noise, God's voice in women's voices is still only a background whisper and often still unheard or diminished.

Perhaps we should not pray for it to be any other way. Perhaps in that marginalization and silencing, God's voice is heard most clearly – if we bother to listen. Perhaps in learning to hear God with a woman's voice, we can all be freed from the pressure and expectation to be loud and overbearing in order to be heard or taken seriously.

However, my prayer is not only for those with a recognized role and responsibility in the churches. Even more I pray that women, and men, will have the grace and gift to voice the love and invitation of God in everyday ways. That, being transforming agents of the Kingdom in the ordinariness of daily life and ready to give account of the hope that is in them, women and men, young and old, will find confidence to be the voice of God for their family, neighbours, colleagues, friends.

I pray that all God's people will be free, every day and all day, having heard God's voice, to give God voice.

Women's voices need to be heard not only as a matter of justice and as a means of building a better society and Church, but because they are central to human flourishing. This book identifies the issues and proclaims that good news.

The Church, each congregation, and wider society need to hear women's voices from the pulpit. Research, initially by Susan Durber and Nicola Slee, for example, suggests that women not only preach differently but also experience faith differently. For the last 40 years women theologians have shown that Scripture is all too often interpreted in male ways, and that women are silenced. The Women's Voices conferences aim to encourage women and men to explore women's role as preachers, to read and hear the Bible as women and to speak and listen from their experiences as women. This book echoes and amplifies those aims, to be both an encouraging and an enabling space.

I'm honoured to be associated with the ongoing work of Women's Voices, and commend this book as it reflects on these early years of the conference and prepares the way for this essential and fruitful work of the Kingdom in the future.

+Libby Lane
Bishop of Derby

Introduction

Almost by chance, a decade ago, I began to teach preaching. At least, I began to assess preaching as part of teaching modules on the Old and New Testaments. The structure both of the modules and the assessment illustrated an important point – that sermons came out of exegeses, and for students were worth only two-thirds of the marks available for the exegetical task. Preaching – inviting the congregation into a biblical passage – was less important than understanding the same passage for yourself, it seemed. Having marked around 500 sermons over ten years I realized that this method of 'teaching' preaching was not working. Despite the variety of preacher, congregation, church tradition and biblical passage, the sermons were generic, multi-purpose and dull. They remained unaffected by the identity of the preacher, the culture of the congregation or the biblical tradition. I began to take teaching preaching much more seriously!

A little later the editor of *The Preacher*, the journal of The College of Preachers, invited me to write an article addressing the question 'Do Women Preach with a Different "Voice"?' More of that in Chapter 2. For now, let me say that the comment of a woman ordinand at the time galvanized me: 'I don't feel I have been taught to preach as myself. I've been taught to preach like a man.'

I was working with a four-source model of theological reflection, and its practical use in biblical interpretation, preaching preparation and classroom learning. This work is published in my book *Straw for the Bricks* (2018). In brief, the method considers two personal sources and two communal sources to explore an issue. The personal sources are Experience and Position (what I believe about something). The communal ones are Tradition (what the Bible or the Church says about the issue) and Culture (what the world in which we live says about it). These sources underpin much of what I will go on to say in this book – you might spot it. Working with these four sources, it seems to me, offers much potential for preachers to identify our own biases, and explore where they come from.

For now, let me introduce myself, and the book.

Me, the preacher

I began preaching in 1994. I loved it. I discovered that I could open up biblical passages in ways that helped people understand them. I could make people laugh, I could make people cry. I could structure sermons that made them engaging and memorable. But over time, I realized I seemed not to be preaching in ways that changed people's lives. No matter how entertaining or informative it might have been, my preaching seemed not to be challenging people to greater discipleship. It wasn't building the body of Christ. I came to the conclusion – reluctantly – that my preaching was failing.

I stopped – for a while. I listened to the hearers of sermons. I thought about what they said. Then, I started again.

This time it was different. I ignored a lot of what I had been taught in homiletics classes, or what I'd read in books on preaching. I ditched my sermon resources. I stopped using illustrations that had never happened to me, or that hadn't happened to me recently.

Then something surprising happened. People began to say they were meeting God in the sermons. One of the best moments I have experienced in ministry came over coffee in the hall of the church where I was serving my curacy. An established member of the congregation came up to me. 'If you're right,' she said, 'then God loves me.' She went away with a smile on her face. And so did I!

Me, the teacher

I have been involved in adult learning for decades. First, I worked outside the Church in further education. One of the most rewarding experiences of my professional life was training women from a socially deprived area to become classroom assistants. The power of learning to transform lives was evident. These women not only learned new things and gained worthwhile employment, in class they shared wisdom gained from life experience – and taught me a lot. I learned another thing too. One very promising student, gifted and dedicated to her learning, arrived on the day of her assessment with no work to present. She arrived with nothing other than tear-stained cheeks for what should have been one of the best days of her life. Her husband, who had failed to come to terms with her learning and gaining a qualification had, overnight, destroyed her work. She experienced a 'situational barrier' to learning (Goodbourn, 1996).

We all learn from a range of sources, way beyond the classroom. Some are identifiable, others are so ingrained in the culture of our family, our community, or our church, that they are difficult to trace. From early on we learn from the way toys are arranged in shops, from the way comments are made about particular behaviours, from the way privileges are bestowed.

Adult learning, whether in a classroom, a homegroup, or from the pulpit, seems to bring with it particular difficulties. Learning something new rarely means simply adding to what we already know. Often it means leaving something else behind – security in our theology or world view, for example. Learning involves loss and turbulence, and is therefore often avoided. Adults can put considerable energy into avoiding situations that disturb their thinking or challenge their beliefs. Such risks are only taken when the risk of not taking the risk is perceived as higher than the risk itself (Hull, 2011).

In almost 30 years of teaching adults, ten of them in the Church, I have perceived some particular difficulties among women learners that have not been present among men – prioritization of a caring role, for example, whether for children or for parents; fitting it in with work and home responsibilities. It is not unusual for potential women candidates for ministry to be asked how they plan to care for their children – a question rarely if ever asked of male candidates.

The book

This book is different! It focuses on how, as women, we might find our own voices, so that *as women* we can contribute to the revelatory act of preaching. I explore reasons why women preachers have a calling to speak honestly as women. Finally, I look at some ways of using our own voices to open hospitable spaces for women and men in our preaching. It is a resource I wish I had had when I first learned to preach, and I pray it will be useful to you. In Chapter 1 we orient our thinking – what is preaching and who is a preacher? Chapter 2 explores how one woman preacher (me!) found her voice. In Chapter 3 we consider how the culture we live in tends towards the silencing of women, and Chapter 4 reflects on how we might hear Bible women's stories. In Chapter 5 we consider how women's experiences of faith and life are distinctive, and how women's faith might develop. Chapter 6 offers some ideas about sermons for women, and Chapter 7 offers a toolkit for developing as a preaching woman. Finally, in Chapter 8 we consider what preaching women might offer the Church.

A good friend, the Revd Dr Kate Bruce, once said that you should never speak or write about preaching without offering examples of your work. The book is peppered with sermon snippets and with whole sermons. I offer them as examples, and not because I am convinced of their excellence.

At the end of each chapter there is a 'Time for reflection'. This is a guided activity, rather than questions to ponder. To make use of it, you will need a quiet, comfortable space where you can think, something to write with and on. I suggest you might journal your way through the book as a means of developing your own preaching.

I

What is Preaching?

This is a book by a woman preacher, for women preachers, about women's preaching. One of my ambitions is to challenge some traditional thinking and practice. While I do want to describe the culture we live in, both within the institution of the Church and in wider society, I do not want to ascribe blame for it to any particular group. I will speak of patriarchy as the dominant narrative we live in, in which a particular male perspective dominates. There are many examples of how this works, some of which we will encounter later. One example is the reporting of an opinion poll on the popularity of Alexandria Ocasio-Cortez, elected to Congress in 2019 and a consistent advocate of social justice. Fox News, CNN and others reported that her approval rating was 'underwater' with *every* group, despite the fact that she had net favourability among all women, all non-white Americans and all 18–34-year-olds. The underlying, patriarchal narrative was that white men of a certain age constitute everybody, thus disenfranchising all women and many men (*Guardian*, 16 March 2019).

At this stage it will be helpful to introduce to you the basis of what comes next – what I believe about preaching and preachers, the strengths and weaknesses, for women, of existing models.

What do we do when we preach?

What is the role of the preacher? What is it we do? Thought showers among ministers and those training for ministry tend to focus on themes of teaching, feeding, inspiring, challenging and comforting. At root such models adopt a 'preacher knows best' stance. Authority might be attributed on the basis of

- knowledge: because the preacher has studied commentaries and read erudite books and worked on the text for some time;
- spirituality: the preacher is speaking the word of God, acting as a mere conduit; or
- position: the preacher is appointed by the Church, or God, to say whatever it is they are about to say.

The assumption is that the preacher knows more than their hearers do about the matter in hand. And so preaching becomes the transmission of knowledge from one person, the one who has it, to other people, the ones who don't. The preacher is at the centre of the preaching model, as disseminator of the word to their hearers. The preacher decides what needs to be said. The preacher chooses what points to make. The preacher decides what might be relevant to those around. The sermon, in this model, is preacher-centric.

It is a patriarchal privileged power paradigm of preaching.

Some preachers seek to be simply channels through which the word of God flows, an invisible conduit that does not contaminate the holy word. But every preacher leaves the vestry in a body, and the congregation sees us as well as hears us. When Jesus summed up the commandments in Matthew 22.37–39 he did not say, 'You must love the Lord your God with all your heart, all your soul, and all your mind ... and love your neighbour.'

He said 'love the Lord your God ... and love your neighbour as your*self*'. He did not suggest that we should erase ourselves from the picture, he said that we have to hold a love of God, neighbour and self in right balance. And he clearly connected loving God with loving both neighbour and self. So we stand to preach not as conduits but as people. One of the wonders of preaching is not that God speaks through human lips, but that God speaks through human personalities.

The Church is not, after all, the idea of Christ, but the body of Christ. We are not meant to embrace Aristotelian philosophy in which the physical is bad and the spiritual is good. We are meant to fully embrace Christian theology in which God became flesh in Christ and remains flesh in his body the Church.

I wonder how often in pastoral situations you have turned to Psalm 139.

> O LORD, you have searched me and known me.
> You know when I sit down and when I rise up; ...
> Even before a word is on my tongue,
>   O LORD, you know it completely. ...
> For it was you who formed my inward parts;
>   you knit me together in my mother's womb. ...
> Search me, O God, and know my heart;
>   test me and know my thoughts.

If, as preachers, we try to disappear from sight, what do we say about the God who made *us*, as well as those to whom we offer pastoral care?

I've taken selected verses here, I know, but let's stick with this psalm just a little longer. Do you notice the tenses? I guess the best-known verse is: 'it was you who formed my inward parts, you knit me together in my mother's womb'. All of that is in the past. There is a tendency among some Christians to build theology on that verse alone – as though God made us before birth but then left us alone to get on with things. For preachers, the outworking of that might be that when we sit down to prepare a sermon – we'll talk more about that later – we have to pray, to invite God into the process. But look at the other verses: 'before a word *is* on my tongue ... you know it completely'; you 'know my heart'; 'test me'.

It's all present, now, current.

It isn't so much that God is going to give us something to say, it's that God has been forming us to say it. Formation is a key element of ministerial training in all denominations, although there might need to be greater acknowledgement of the fact that it begins before selection and training and continues after it. Alongside formation sits the concept of calling. Again, it might erroneously be viewed as a one-off event. And a 'call' to ministry is often seen as a generic call to all that ministry, whether authorized, licensed or ordained, might include. What a difference it would make, I believe, if we thought ourselves called to preach – sent 'to the Scripture on behalf of [our] community' to 'hear a particular word for them on this day and in this place' (Long, 1988: 50). We are sent, you are sent, by your congregation to this text on this day to find treasure for them.

What is a sermon?

Before moving on, let's decide what it is we are talking about. What do we mean by 'sermon'? What definition will we work with for the remainder of this book?

Moltmann, Brueggemann and Long among others acknowledge three ingredients in the sermon – the preacher, the hearers and either God or the Bible, depending on whose model you choose. The relationships between the three differ according to homiletic theory. The preaching role might be to declare – to get the message straight and to get it said; it might be to advise – to hear the problems of the congregation and answer them from Scripture; it might be to inform – to tell the congregation what needs to be believed; it might be to entertain. Each has significant problems. Concern with getting something said can fail to work on getting it heard. Starting with the congregation can render sermons little more than therapy. Information-giving assumes that the preacher has a once-and-for-all grasp of the truth. Entertainment can best be found elsewhere. Such models may have particular problems for women preachers, too. As we will see later, women preachers have unique problems in being heard, whether we try to proclaim or to teach, and many of us have experienced problems in being regarded

4

as authoritative, even when we are! We are often expected to be pastoral or therapeutic in what we say.

Some preachers seek a halfway house between teaching and pastoring. The preacher exegetes the passage, works out how to communicate it and then thinks of how it might be relevant to the hearers. As a sermon it has two parts, explanation of the passage followed by application. It is a poor method. Which of us really understands the lives of our hearers? Relevance, it seems to me, is a value preachers often espouse but rarely practice. It can be tyrannical, imposing a requirement first to invent and then to hit targets that somehow relate to the individual lives of our hearers.

An alternative metaphor of preaching, offered by Tom Long (1988), is the preacher as witness. Authority does not rest on position or knowledge, but on what the preacher has experienced of God. As witness the preacher highlights the actions of God in the world, the church and the community. We are called to present what we know in persuasive and convincing ways.

I define preaching as 'the art of engaging the people of God in their shared narrative by creatively and hospitably inviting them into an exploration of biblical text, by means of which, corporately and individually, they might encounter the divine'. Here, the preacher is host. The table to which people are invited has been carefully laid, taking into account who will be there and what they need. A meal has been carefully selected and meticulously prepared. It is both a communal and a personal event. Guests are welcomed in, conversation will flow – sometimes among just a few, sometimes as community. It will be a unique experience for all.

What is preaching for women?

As I said earlier, we stand to preach not as conduits but as people. As a woman preacher, I have found the idea of preacher as declarer of truth, possessing words from God to be delivered direct, hard to espouse. As writers such as Copeland (2014), Lawless (2015) and Gross (2017) have attested, the culture of many congregations expects truth to be wrapped in male bodies, pronounced in masculine terms. As a result, women embody the Word differently from men from the outset.

We are shaped by gender, through a history that is 'but the biography of great men' (Carlyle, 1841),[1] in biblical commentaries that largely occlude women's contributions, and often in front of congregations dubious of our right to be standing before them. Our 'embodied presence will impart meaning to the preaching event through both the speaking and the hearing before [we] ever utter[s] a word' (Copeland, 2014: 67). So, whether intentionally or otherwise, women preachers preach differently, because we are heard differently. Despite the claims of some that we ought not to appear in our sermons, we already do. It is our body standing at the front of the church. It is our voice saying the words. It is our understanding we share.

Our presence in our preaching is foundational to this book. Since we are present in our sermons, we need to acknowledge it, and wrestle with how best to be there. Failure to acknowledge subjectivity implies that my opinions, or beliefs or convictions are 'truth', and that anyone who disagrees is mistaken or wrong. I was taught not to use phrases such as 'I think' or 'in my experience' in case they put me into the sermon. The fact, I think, is that we talk about ourselves all the time, because that's whose shoes we wear. We have interpreted the Bible in light of our own experiences and impressions and beliefs. Whatever we say about a Bible passage it will be influenced by our own attitudes and thoughts. Even if we deliver a sermon straight from a commentary, it is influenced by our own beliefs – the belief that the commentator has better insight into Scripture than we do; or that academic reading is more important than devotional; or that I have nothing to say.

Isaiah 49.1–2 describes how God prepares us to speak:

The LORD called me before I was born,
while I was in my mother's womb he named me.

He made my mouth like a sharp sword,
    in the shadow of his hand he hid me;
he made me a polished arrow,
    in his quiver he hid me away.

If we are called to preach by God and sent to our text by the congregation these verses suggest God has made us effective communicators. God hid us in God's hand and polished us like arrows. God hid us in God's quiver. A lot of that takes place unseen, in the shadow, in the quiver. Yet it is that work of God that makes us sharp and polished. It is our experience that forms our understanding of God and gives us something to say to others that only we can say.

When Jesus healed the man with demons and restored him to his right mind, the man wanted to leave town and go with the other disciples to follow Jesus. But Jesus said 'No'.

Why?

Because only *that* man could tell *that* story to *those* people. When Jesus revisited the region, multitudes came out to meet him. Our life experience equips us to tell our story so that others might come to Jesus. The easiest sermon preparation in the world is to go to a study Bible or commentary, pick out a bit we like and pass it on. It may also be the most stress-inducing preparation in the world. If our reflex action is to read as much as possible before preaching, rather than starting from our own experience, we pile up work for ourselves. If God is forming, shaping and preparing us, our starting point can be what we have experienced and understood.

Situated knowledge, experience, is an important starting point for interpreting the world (Durber, 2007). This kind of knowledge is rooted in who we are, what we have learned and from where. It took a breastfeeding mother to draw my attention to Exodus 2.2 before I really appreciated it. Moses' mother kept him quiet for three months before hiding him in the bulrushes! Experience can highlight things that are more often hidden. Worthwhile sermons often come from real experience.

I think we see them in three Old Testament figures.

When God commissioned Moses, what did he do? God appeared to Moses in a burning bush. If you were to walk through your nearest gardens and a bush was burning, you would notice it. But Moses was in the desert. The bushes were dry. There was nothing really unusual about a burning bush. What was unusual was Moses' curiosity. The first attribute a good preacher needs to develop is curiosity, the art of noticing things. This alone will enable a woman to preach differently from a man. We tend to notice different things, particularly if we are concerned about women's rights. I will return to this point later in Chapter 3, so bear with me for now. At a celebration of partial women's suffrage in Manchester, in 2018 the audience was asked a series of questions to illustrate how life experience differs between women and men. 'Who has ever got their car key into their hand so they can get into the car as quickly as possible at night?' Almost every woman stood. 'Who checks what they are wearing to see whether it might be misinterpreted by a member of the opposite sex?' More women stood. 'Who constantly looks behind them if they are walking home alone?' Some men this time. If truth is forged from experience, and I believe it is, the truths forged differ for men and for women. The calling of every preacher is to notice, a bit like a child wandering along a beach. As you go about your ordinary business, you collect all kinds of things – a few shells, a bit of stick, an interesting bit of driftwood. When you come to preach you sort through your collection and take out what seems appropriate to the passage you are to speak on.

That practice has two effects. By relating your own experience of God to your everyday life, you are saying to your hearers, 'the word of God is a living thing'. You are also saying, 'God can be found in the everyday.'

As well as the curiosity of a Moses, we need determination.

Of the three Hebrew patriarchs, Abraham, Isaac and Jacob, the people of God were named after only one of them, Jacob, who became Israel. He became Israel *not* because he obeyed, *not* because he served, *not* because he worshipped, but because he wrestled. He wrestled with God and would not let go without a blessing (Gen. 32.22–32). God named his people after the one who struggled for a blessing, who wouldn't let go. I think that's part of our calling as preachers too. The plethora of online commentaries enables us to duck out of this fight too easily. Rather than wrestle until we see something for ourselves, we give way to our insecurities and look up what someone else has said. Or worse, we move away from the lectionary (a three-year cycle of readings used by the majority of mainline churches) and choose sermon series which enable us either to base several weeks of preaching on one source, or to stick within our own comfort zones. When Jacob wrestled with God he was alone, having sent his companions and his possessions across the river. We too must learn to be alone with Scripture, standing as ourselves, with our weaknesses, biases and responses, and wrestle until we are blessed with a word for ourselves and our hearers. As Tom Long has said, 'preaching is a wild river, wide and deep' (1998: 12). Sticking to the shallows or sharing someone else's account of the crossing cheats both ourselves and our congregations out of blessing. Our own understanding of faith is simply a wave on the shore. Our congregations need to swim depths.

Moses was curious, Jacob determined and, as a model for women preachers, I want to suggest that Queen Vashti was aware. On first reading the book of Esther, Vashti seems only to have a bit part. By the end of the first chapter, she is gone. Her contribution, though, is significant. At the start of the story both she and the king are hosting banquets, boozy ones. On the seventh day of the banquet, 'when the king was merry with wine' (Esth. 1.10), Ahasuerus sends for Vashti 'in order to show the peoples and the officials her beauty' (11). The king is drunk, as will be his guests. He summons Vashti away from her own guests because he wants to show off her beauty to other men. He treats her as a possession, he treats her guests with disdain, and in such a highly charged atmosphere who knew what might happen – in all likelihood, he puts her at risk. Vashti refuses to go.

The king's concern is not for her, but for his own position. He consults his lawyers (13). There follows a magnificent patriarchal narrative which results in Vashti's dismissal:

'Not only has Queen Vashti done wrong to the king, but also to all the officials and all the peoples who are in all the provinces of King Ahasuerus. For this deed of the queen will be made known to all women, causing them to look with contempt on their husbands, since they will say, "King Ahasuerus commanded Queen Vashti to be brought before him, and she did not come." This very day the noble ladies of Persia and Media who have heard of the queen's behaviour will rebel against the king's officials, and there will be no end of contempt and wrath! If it pleases the king, let a royal order go out from him, and let it be written among the laws of the Persians and the Medes so that it may not be altered, that Vashti is never again to come before King Ahasuerus; and let the king give her royal position to another who is better than she. So when the decree made by the king is proclaimed throughout all his kingdom, vast as it is, all women will give honour to their husbands, high and low alike.' (1.16–20)

In other words, if Queen Vashti gets away with standing up to her husband, all the women will be doing it!

What did Vashti do? She saw what was happening and was honest about it. Had she prevailed, other women would have gained the courage to speak out against injustice too. But Vashti does not achieve nothing. Ahasuerus may have learned something from this incident, for when Esther takes the risk of going to see him, unsummoned, she is welcomed. When she speaks she is heard.

An example of wrestling

I avoid speaking or writing about preaching without giving examples of my own sermons. What follows is an example of wrestling. I was guest speaker at a large church with a vicar I greatly respect. I wanted to preach well, in other words. The passage was one I had usually avoided, if given the option. To me it did not make sense. Over a period of a couple of months, I read and reread Mark 9.33–37. Jesus and his disciples have just arrived in Capernaum. The disciples have been arguing, and Jesus asks them what about. Then he gets a child and places it among the group. I discovered key ideas I could work with. The status of children at the time of the story, for example, and the fact that we don't really know what the disciples were arguing about. Then I decided on an experience where I had noticed something similar to part of this narrative.

This is the full sermon:

Sermon

A couple of weeks ago I took my nearly two-year-old grandson to Dunham Massey deer park. It all looked very promising. The sun was shining and as we got into the park area a group of deer had already emerged from the woods and children slightly older than T were hand-feeding them leaves and branches. I thought that would entertain him for a while. But it wasn't what T wanted. He made it clear he wanted to move on.

The thing was that earlier this year I had taken him there with his two older cousins. And on that occasion the deer had not come out of hiding, but had remained in the trees and difficult to spot. The children had had great fun finding deer among the trees that others simply walked past.

Clearly T wanted to repeat the experience and so we set off through the park to the remotest end, and then began walking back as quietly as a one-year-old can manage.

Sure enough, though, T found some deer. And he was very pleased with himself. What was even more striking was that other people walked past, without seeing the deer that we were watching.

It made me think about today's reading.

In the interests of full disclosure I have to tell you that I struggled to make much sense of this set of circumstances that Mark relates

---

here. And I certainly found it hard to understand why he chose to tell this story to the church he was writing to.

Mark wrote to Christians in Rome. They were having a hard time. A large fire had destroyed part of the city. The emperor was looking for someone to blame and chose the immigrants – the Jews. To protect themselves the Jews chose an even smaller minority and passed the blame onto them. The asylum seekers got the blame – the Jewish Christians. As a result Roman soldiers wandered through the ghetto day after day hunting them down and killing not just the men and women but the children too.

For people who had chosen to follow a risen saviour and triumphant lord, these must have been particularly difficult circumstances.

Even the disciples in the story were having a difficult time. Jesus had told them that he was going to be betrayed and executed but would rise again. And despite the fact that they had only recently, according to Mark, seen Jesus cast out an evil spirit, and before that some of them had been up a mountain and seen Jesus with Moses and Elijah and heard the voice of God say Jesus was his beloved son, they were confused and worried. Where could God be in a scenario where Jesus was going to die? That idea was totally foreign to them – gods most certainly did not die.

We don't really know what the disciples argued about on the road: 'Who was the greatest' might mean which of them was most important; or whether Jesus really could defeat death; whether the Romans really could execute someone God called his Son; or even which of them would manage to be faithful through the coming trials. Probably these reflect the kind of arguments going on in the church in Rome, where some Christians admitted their faith and were killed, while others denied it in order to save their families.

We do know that they were embarrassed about their quarrel because when Jesus asks what it was about, they don't answer. In Mark's Gospel Jesus and the disciples are always on the road to Jerusalem, always on the path of pilgrimage – as all of Jesus' followers always have been and still are. On this occasion they stop off in Capernaum, apparently in an ordinary household. Jesus gathers them around him and addresses their question, 'Whoever wants to be first must be last of all and servant of all.' That sounds great – so great that management books and training courses have hijacked it to talk about successful leadership in business and commerce. But I think it has been hijacked because it seems to have been interpreted in ways that have led to Christians falling over themselves to serve in order that everybody knows how important they are in the commonwealth of God.

And then Jesus puts the child among them and talks about welcoming a child.

It struck me that had my grandson been older and maybe had a camera or binoculars with him the people who passed by without seeing the deer at Dunham the other week might have had the privilege of watching them play and feed and approach of their own volition. But because it was a one-year-old and his grandmother they probably assumed we weren't looking at anything. And they missed out.

What is it about this child?

Again it seems to me that the collective wisdom of the Church has ensured that many have a very firm grasp of the wrong end of the stick. We think if we welcome children then Jesus will be among us, and not only Jesus but the one who sent him.

I'm not sure our attention should be on the child alone. Jesus took the child and put it among them. Is it the 'among them' that is significant?

A week or so ago a Facebook friend requested prayers for someone from their church who was going overseas to work as a missionary. They asked that people would pray that they would take Jesus with them.

I was pretty sure that they would find he was already there when they arrived!

Could it be that the disciples wondered where God was going to be as his Son was betrayed and killed? Could it be that the Christians in Rome wondered where he was as they were betrayed and executed?

And Jesus was saying, 'I'm here – in the midst of you, among the overlooked, the neglected, the excluded, the inconsequential, the unconsidered, the worthless.'

Just over a year ago our daughter was very seriously ill. One day we received a phone call, 'Get in a taxi now, don't stop to collect anything, tell the driver to get you here as quickly as possible.'

When we arrived our daughter couldn't breathe – the illness that had robbed her of her strength was closing down her lungs, and she was suffocating. A variety of medics moved round the room with tubes and pipes and machines. Our daughter said goodbye to us.

Just before she lost consciousness I looked up and there was the associate rector from her church walking into the room. It was a split-second thing – the timing was precise.

Later she told us that she had been at the desk in her study planning her day when she felt an 'urging', a bit of a nudge, to go to the hospital *now*. She got into her car – where she could neither answer the phone nor respond to emails. Because of traffic and roadworks it took her 40 minutes to do what was actually a ten-minute journey. And she arrived at exactly the right time.

An insignificant urge – and it felt miraculous to us.

One of my favourite writers, Barbara Brown Taylor, tells of wondering how she could change her world for good, allow people she met a glimpse of God. Again, it was simple, she decided just to say 'bless you' to people when she said goodbye. She said it to the checkout woman at the supermarket. Apparently they were the kindest words that person heard all day.

I think what the disciples and the early Christians in Rome might have been doing was something that I certainly do, and I guess that you do too. Looking for God in our everyday lives.

And yet the accumulated insight of those wise about the spiritual life suggests that the reason so many of us cannot see the X that marks the spot of God's presence is because we are standing on it. The treasure we seek requires no lengthy expedition, no expensive equipment, no superior aptitude or special company. All we lack is the willingness to imagine that we already have everything we need. Among the insignificant and unimportant and everyday we are already in the presence of God. The only thing missing is our ability to see it.

Why the child?

We show hospitality to strangers not merely because they need it, but because we need it, too. This child is the living symbol and memory that we are all strangers here. This is not our house, our table, our food, our lodging; this is God's house and table and food and lodging. We, like the disciples, and like those early

Christians in Rome, are pilgrims and wanderers, aliens and strangers, but we are welcome in this place. To welcome the child is to say we too have weaknesses, uncertainties and insecurities, yet grace, in us and through us, will surprise us all.

Note

1 Carlyle is primarily credited with the 'great man' theory of history, a nineteenth-century idea that explained history in terms of the impact of heroes.

2

Finding My Voice

Learning to preach

I think I have felt called to preach for as long as I can remember. Initially, however, I recognized this more as an unfulfillable desire than a call. The theology espoused by my church, and the Christian groups I was part of, was clear that women did not preach. My theology taught me that my yearning was wrong. Being part of a university Christian Union reinforced this view, backing it up with some ostensibly Bible-based teaching. Later I spent many a Sunday morning listening to sermons that seemed irrelevant, or demeaning – how many jokes told by preachers are at the expense of women, I wonder.

Living with frustration seemed to be part of female discipleship.

Eventually I became a youth leader. In the group was a young person who was far less tolerant of the idea of a God who both gifts and denies women. Despite the fact that the Church of England did not yet ordain women, she was convinced of her call and determined to pursue it. When she shared this with me, I had a dilemma. It became a greater dilemma when another member of the church told me I needed to correct her – 'women don't teach men'. The source of the prohibition was allegedly the Bible, so I decided to turn to it. The most difficult text, from my perspective, seemed to be 1 Timothy 2.11–15:

Let a woman learn in silence with full submission. I permit no woman to teach or to have authority over a man; she is to keep silent. For Adam was formed first, then Eve; and Adam

16

was not deceived, but the woman was deceived and became a transgressor. Yet she will be saved through childbearing, provided they continue in faith and love and holiness, with modesty.

It is an apparently difficult passage from a woman's perspective, unless, as some suggest, the emphasis is on 'let women learn' rather than on silence and submission. Silence, anyway, is better interpreted as quietness (Keener, 1993).

In the end the passage sent me to the Genesis story of Adam and Eve. The story seems to suggest that woman was made to be man's assistant (Gen. 2.18). Interpretation hangs on the word translated helper – *ezer*. It is used 15 times in the Hebrew Scriptures, and 14 times it refers to God, as in Psalm 30.10 'O LORD, be my helper', and Psalm 54.4 'surely, God is my helper'. The *ezer* was meant to be 'suitable'. The word translated suitable is *knegedu*, a word not found anywhere else in the Bible. It comes from the root *neged*, which means 'standing boldly opposite'. In other words God did not make the woman to be man's maid, but his partner, standing eye to eye with him.

Women seemed to be well hidden in the Bible. Only 1.2 per cent of biblical text is spoken by a woman, and only 49 named women speak, yet they are often surprisingly bold, striding onto the page with 'heads held high and hearts full of passion' (Freeman, 2014).

I read Elaine Storkey's *What's Right with Feminism?* (1989) and later Michelle Guinness' *Woman the Full Story* (2003). There was enough evidence in my studies to change my mind.

Some time later, I became a Reader in the Church of England, and was subsequently ordained.

I loved preaching. Members of the congregation were more than affirming. One of them, a talented dramatist, gave me perhaps one of the most significant gifts anyone can ever give a new preacher. He offered to listen to all my sermons for a period of three years, and to give me proper, critical feedback. I quickly accepted. His notes on a 20-minute sermon would run to four and five pages on everything from theological content to pitch, pace and pause. I was learning to become a preacher, and feeling fulfilled.

Yet, despite the generous support, my enthusiasm, and the esteem in which my church held the sermon, I still preached in a way similar to the one with which I was familiar; like the preachers I had heard and occasionally admired. In other words, like a man. I would present a rational argument in a structured way with an introduction, three points beginning with the same letter, and a conclusion. I have since discovered that this is not naturally my way of speaking, although it is neither necessarily masculine nor wrong.

My underlying assumptions and attitudes were rooted in the patriarchal culture of the day. I would often start with a joke. Sadly, almost all jokes are at someone else's expense, and many of those contained in joke books for preachers are profoundly sexist. I made assumptions about biblical women that were common at the time and in the context – they were almost all weak or sinful. This had the effect, unrealized at the time, of distancing me, as well as other women, from the women in the Bible. It seemed there were few of them, if any, I would want to emulate. And so, even as a woman, the heroes of the faith I presented to my hearers were almost uniquely male. Even when the Virgin Mary got a look in during Advent, the version I presented was Mrs Alexander's meek and mild mother[1] rather than the revolutionary herald of Luke's Gospel.

Becoming aware

After ordination I preached regularly and was an enthusiastic recruit to the teaching of homiletics when the opportunity arose.

I remained unaware of the underlying patriarchal bias in my own preaching until I was asked, in 2014, to write an article for *The Preacher*, the journal of The College of Preachers, on the subject of women's preaching. Walking through Berkley Square in London after a meeting, the editor asked me whether

I thought women had a different preaching 'voice' from men. After brief thought I indicated that I did. 'Could you write 1,800 words on that?' he asked.

That was it. A few moments' thought and 1,800 words changed my preaching life!

I contacted some women preachers I knew, and some I didn't know but had read. I asked as many students training for ordained ministry in the Church of England as I could (I spent a residential weekend with 60 of them). I read as many books as possible in the short space of time I had available. The research and reading I did for the article disquieted my practice and challenged my perspectives. The most disturbing response I received to the question, 'Do women preach with a different voice?' was 'I haven't been taught to preach as myself. I've been taught to preach like a man.' It's a comment that has stayed with me, and inspired much of the work I have since done. It is a comment that has inspired this book.

This is the article:[2]

Do women preach with a different 'voice'?

'Jesus calls us to be fishers of men,' declaimed the preacher to a somewhat bemused baptism congregation. Being fishers was not an image that sprang immediately to mind, other than perhaps angling by the side of the local lake. But more importantly, what might 'fishing for men' mean to the rather attractive, well-dressed woman who was now addressing them? The very fact that the phrase was lifted from one of the Gospels and repeated by a woman without too much thought caused confusion in the minds of the hearers.

Whether or not women preach with a different voice from men, the fact that the preacher is a woman can mean that the message is heard differently. Dissonance between message and messenger results in hidden meanings being transmitted, as well as what is actually spoken.

The key question for preachers, however, is, 'Is it delivered differently?'

Christianity, from the beginning, has been an incarnated faith. Some will say that it was incarnated in Jesus, God in the form of a man, and that it should therefore continue to be incarnated in men. This is not the place to enter that debate. Suffice it to say that I write from the perspective of a faith incarnated in all, men and women, who seek to follow Christ. Indeed, I would argue that unless the faith is incarnated in women too, it is only presented in part to those around.

There are two interlinked questions about women's preaching: do women preach with a different 'voice' from men? And should we?

Ask a group of 60 or so students training for ordained and licensed ministries, who therefore spend a great deal of time listening to, preparing and evaluating preaching, and the response is a resounding 'yes', though few could articulate the reason for their answer.

A quick literature review yields little fruit, with the vast majority from America, where the history of women preaching is very different. While books about women's ministry through the ages, women in mission and feminist interpretations of difficult texts abound, there is little that encourages women to develop a style that is true to their sex. Susan Durber published *Preaching Like a Woman* in 2007, some time ago now, in which she argues for a deliberately feminist approach to preaching and presents several of her own sermons. Since then innovative work has been thin on the ground, and some of the writing done on women in ministry has avoided speaking of preaching.

Whether or not women's preaching is in some way distinctive is often addressed with certain trepidation. Feminists seem to suggest that women should consciously preach differently, in order to reclaim space defined and held by men. Conservatives (of both catholic and evangelical persuasion) tend to avoid an answer in the affirmative in case it might challenge the authority of Church or Scripture. Perceived differences are therefore more likely to be attributed to personality type than to gender.

Both approaches carry significant risk. If a sermon is about relating Word to world for the present congregation, to what extent might a conscious intent to claim back occupied territory compromise the preacher, the sermon or even the Scripture? And what should be the authority balance between Scripture and feminist critique? On the other hand, denying difference between sexes by attributing all difference to personality smacks of a secular individualism anathema to the community of the church, while also ignoring all we know about collective memory and shared experience.

Conscious and unconscious difference

Women do seem to preach with a different voice from men, whether intentionally or otherwise. They communicate differently. Even Elizabeth Aries (*Men and Women in Interaction*, 1996), who questioned the widely accepted research on this, came to the conclusion that while not all women communicated differently from all men, the sexes did exhibit different tendencies; they come to faith differently (Nicola Slee, *Women's Faith Development*, 2004); their life experience is different. Each of these characteristics will influence the way women preach.

Women's unconscious voice might include a tendency towards narrative rather than apologetic preaching (on average women use 20,000 words a day, while men use only 7,000); greater focus on stories and illustrations from everyday life; vulnerability – but only if women are encouraged to preach authentically, rather than to emulate the preaching of male colleagues or lecturers.

Of course, unconscious communication is not always positive, and the preacher who feels that they are on 'foreign' territory or have no right to be where they are will, at least in part, communicate as much to their hearers. Equally, the woman who from childhood has learned to win approval by 'girlish' behaviour might unconsciously fall into that when preaching.

It is when women preach consciously as women that they have the most to offer. Durber suggests that women use preaching to reclaim ground (the pulpit) that has traditionally belonged to men. From a feminist perspective such a view has much to recommend it. I believe that there are more important reasons for women to preach as women. First, women's joint experience is of life in a patriarchal society; as members of the less powerful group. While men are able to preach about marginalization from an academic perspective, in Britain it is very difficult for a male preacher to preach with authenticity about the experience of being marginalized. For most women preachers, powerlessness will have been lived at one level or another. When the preacher identifies this honestly, the gospel is more likely to sound real to those in the pew.

A wider perspective on Scripture

Second, women reading Scripture self-consciously as women should find much material there that is hidden from men readers. Google sermons on David and Bathsheba, for example, and you will likely find many that portray David as weak, in the wrong place at the wrong time, and even Bathsheba as a temptress. Few pick up on the key words 'she was cleansing herself after her period' (2 Sam. 11.4 NRSV). Bathsheba was obeying the religious law when the king called for her because he wanted to have sex with her. Even the story of the death of the child who follows this act is usually told from the man's perspective. Women preachers should be in a position to fully explore stories such as this and gain from them comfort for those who are abused and oppressed. In other ways, the exploration of what is really happening in biblical texts, particularly to those on the edges of the story, should encourage women to see their own value to God. The Church has too long promoted a gospel in which men are the heroes and women the ill, weak or sinful. Preaching that regularly explores events from a liminal perspective should encourage Christians to develop a more enquiring mindset when approaching Scripture.

The problem, of course, is that colleges and courses training people for ministry do not train women as preachers distinct from men. Perhaps the larger problem is that courses on preaching are predominantly taught by men, and the masculine approach is deemed to be the 'norm'. There is a danger of depending on the structure of sermons as communication and slotting preachers into them, instead of recognizing and developing the strengths and communication styles of the sexes and exploring ways of using them to full effect in preaching. Again, I do not envisage a dualistic divide, but a spectrum or tendencies and experiences.

Preaching that speaks to women (and men)

My third point is probably the most contentious. Sermons based on a patriarchal view of spirituality and discipleship tend to focus on masculine weaknesses, while feminine failures are seldom mentioned. Typically, we might hear pride and selfishness denounced and care for others promoted – and many women in the congregation will not feel challenged, because they can point to the number of others they care for.

Margaret Guenther (1992: 134) says, 'The time I have spent listening to women's stories has convinced me that there are distinctly feminine patterns of sinfulness, and that pride is not women's besetting sin ... even as they talk of pride they are feeling worthless and powerless.' Saiving (1960: 108) suggests that 'temptations of woman as woman are not the same as the temptations of man as man'. At any rate, there is sufficient evidence to suggest that the widely accepted definition of sin as prideful does not match the experience spiritual directors and theologians have of women.

A sermon addressing these issues might deal quite differently with Romans 12.3 than one approaching the text from a purely androcentric perspective. 'Thinking of oneself with sober judgement,' might mean recognizing strengths as well as identifying weaknesses.

Slee (2004: 40) found that the 'majority [of women] offered explicitly relational models of faith ... understanding faith as being in relation with God and/or the Other'. They are more likely to think of sin as broken relationship rather than specific wrongdoing. In a recent TED[3] talk, Rita Pierson spoke of the importance of authentic relationship in order to support development. She was speaking of children, but the same is likely to be true of adults, that we only really learn from those we feel we know and can trust. If preachers hide behind their words rather than reveal something of themselves, hearers are unlikely to detect the authenticity they seek. Paul was able to say 'be imitators of me' because the Christians at Corinth had got to know him. Preaching that appeals to women, and is true to female tendencies, is perhaps more relational than academic (although sound study should stand behind it), taking hearers on a journey through the passage, rather than presenting propositions about it, and including aspects of the preacher's own faith.

Unless preachers, particularly women preachers, get to grips with preaching about the experiences of women, the faith will not be truly embodied for the whole community. While women, I believe, should preach as women they should avoid speaking only to women. The aim should be to image God better by preaching, and hearing, human, gendered sermons rather than androgynous sermons aimed at homogenous congregations. This will benefit both women and men, by allowing them to enter into each others' experience and understanding of God, maybe by opening Scripture differently, and by offering a bigger picture of the One we seek to follow.

Do women preach with a different voice from men? I think so. Should they do so? Yes, for the sake of a holistically incarnated gospel. The next question might be 'Should churches and training institutions do anything about it?'

Knowing my place

The response led to our inaugural conference, Women's Voices, in the Diocese of Chester. It is testament to the desire for such an event that while the first conference relied on sponsorship from four organizations, it has since taken on a life and identify of its own.

Rereading my 2014 article a few years later, I notice my own absence. I present and expound three arguments that support my thesis that women do preach with a different voice. I recruit evidence from published works to support it. I draw a conclusion that scarcely challenges:

> Do women preach with a different voice from men? I think so. Should they do so? Yes, for the sake of a holistically incarnated gospel. The next question might be 'Should churches and training institutions do anything about it?'

It is as though I am hiding behind the voices of others. Partly, I suspect, I was taught to write in that way from grammar school onwards. But I also detect a fear of stating clearly what I believe, and of acknowledging my own experience. Although I tried to be anonymous in the article, many of the responses to it felt very personal, and although I had not set out to write vulnerably, I felt exposed by dismissive comments such as, 'Just the sort of unequal thinking rife in the world of feminism.' I had tried, gently, to adjust what I saw as an imbalance, and was summarily dismissed.

In his book *Inclusivity: A Gospel Mandate* (2015), Diarmuid O'Murchu borrowed the title of an essay by Gayatri Chakravorty Spivak (1994), 'Can the Subaltern Speak?' In it the subaltern is not overtly oppressed but is without representative voice. O'Murchu suggests that an oppressive invisibility – subaltern status – can attach to ethnicity, gender, disability and any way of being different from the dominant culture, even though there may be no obvious oppression. In other words, he, and Spivak, are speaking of those to whom nobody listens, or whom nobody sees. Returning briefly to the previous chapter, these are the people who are omitted when preachers submit to the tyranny of relevance.

'Subaltern' is the name Spivak gave to those who, while not overtly oppressed, have no voice. Yet, she asserted, 'the oppressed ... *if given the chance* ... can speak' (italics mine). How might this happen? Spivak was working in the world of academia. She charged female academics to take seriously their opportunity to critique existing power structures as a means of giving voice for the silenced. In other words, members of subaltern groups who do have a voice should use it to somehow represent those members of the same group who do not. The same can, and should, be said of other silenced groups (ethnic minorities, people with disabilities, members of disenfranchised communities). This book is about women, and women's preaching, but I believe some of the principles we explore apply equally well to members of other silenced groups.

O'Murchu's thesis is that subaltern status exists in both public and religious spheres. He considers it from the perspective of Christian thinking. The idea of being a Chosen People is oppressive in itself, he says, since being Chosen also bestows privilege and power, and necessitates the existence of the 'not-Chosen'. Christianity's obsession with 'Chosen-ness', he claims, can be traced back to 'Constantine's addiction to patriarchal power'. Chosen-ness is inherent in power structures, no matter who does the choosing. In patriarchal structures it is men who are chosen and women who are not.

Central to my desire to preach as myself, as a woman, is the belief that traditional Christianity has, down the centuries, silenced the voices of women. As members of a subaltern group who have nevertheless been given a voice, I believe the challenge to speak out is apposite. I believe that women preachers should preach as women. It is part of the pursuit of an incarnated, or embodied, Christian faith shared through preaching and teaching. Embodiment simply means denying the Greek philosophy that body is bad and spirit is good, and accepting that we experience life through our whole bodies. What we experience can challenge what we have learned from church tradition. It is particularly important for women preachers, because the fact of being a female body means being seen and heard differently.

After the republication of my article, and the receipt of feedback essentially telling me to be quiet, I identified myself as subaltern, a member of a group that does not contribute to the hegemonic narrative but rather is silenced by it. Realizing my place in this group was important. In preaching, it finally rid me of any tendency to preach *to* the congregation, and prompted me to think in terms of preaching *from* it, as one of a group often silenced.

In writing 'Do Women Preach with a Different "Voice"?' and planning the Women's Voices conference, I had fallen into the 'rescuer trap'. I had seen the problem, I was going to do something about it, and I was going to help other women. Realizing my own subaltern status radically changed this attitude. I had seen the problem. I was going to do something. But from within.

Keys to my development

My article proposed three ways in which women's preaching is different from the male norm:

- our experience of life is different and, being seen as women, we are heard differently;
- if we read the Bible as women, we will see different things in it from male readers;
- women's faith and women's sin is distinctive, and preaching as a woman will allow us to speak more directly to women.

In the summary I said women should preach as women 'for the sake of a holistically incarnated gospel'.

Change does not happen overnight, and the implications of my new perspectives are taking time to work out. My homiletics education propounded a generic preaching theory, largely based on 'preacher knows best'. I am working out from this to a new paradigm, based on my own Experience and emerging Position.

A key question all preachers, but particularly women preachers, need to answer concerns the interaction between experience and theological conviction. As a young person my experience of feeling called to preach was subjugated to my theology that God didn't want women to preach. Now I value experience as a valid means of interrogating theology. I also regard it as essential to effective preaching. As a preacher I am no longer a proclaimer of dispassionate truth, but a witness of what I have seen God do. I do not need to look only to the authority of tradition or the Church, each of which is inherently sexist; nor do I need to prioritize what biblical studies tutors call 'commentary work'. Preaching is becoming, to a certain extent, testimony.

Speaking *from* experience has long been valued by preachers such as Tom Long: 'Before a preacher *says* something a preacher must *see* something. To be a preacher is to be called to be a *witness,* one who sees before speaking, one whose right to speak has been created by what has been seen' (1988: 4). Writing in *Preaching Like a Woman* (2007: 5), Susan Durber encourages women preachers to 'value the truths we forge from our own experience and declare such "situated knowledge" a starting point for interpreting the world'. Likewise, preaching *for* experience has been valued by writers such as Leonard Sweet: 'The core issue of preaching is not "getting something said"; it is not even "getting something heard"; it is getting something experienced that can transform your life for God and the gospel' (2014: 46)

But is there such a thing as 'women's experience', and how might it be identified?

I do not want to say, I do not believe, that women are inherently one thing or another, or that we are essentially likely to do this or that, but I am prepared to situate women's lives in a common sphere dominated by patriarchal narrative in which we are likely to encounter similar problems. Recent initiatives such as the #MeToo campaign, Laura Bates' everyday sexism project and the community art work Eva's Call,[4] a response to the 'Nevertheless she Persisted' movement, are testament to that. Similarly, women preachers step into a space, the pulpit, that has been occupied and defined by men for centuries.

My experience is that being a woman affects the way my preaching is heard, and affects the way I read the Bible in preparing to preach. My position is that experience matters theologically and personally. I, as everyone else, experience life holistically through body and mind, though I am often judged only on my body. In experiencing the world as it is I have something in common with other women. My responses to that experience are personal, other women respond differently. In preaching from my own experience as a woman I have not only 'common' experience but also my self to share. It is the combination of the two that avoids assumptions that everyone feels as I do, and that all feel the same (essentialism and generalization).

The three key points from my article (life experience, Bible reading and distinctive spiritual experiences) transitioned into the themes I now work with: embodiment, self and voice.

Embodiment

Embodiment has been in sharp focus through much of my thinking. Lacking the language of feminist practical theology at the time, I wrote in 2014 'from the perspective of a faith incarnated in all, men and women, who seek to follow Christ'. It is a double-edged concept. If a woman consciously ignores or rejects the idea that she is embodied as a woman, she lives, and preaches, a disembodied faith that struggles to be incarnational. Here the gospel suffers, because it becomes separated from lived faith. When a woman preacher fails to acknowledge or address the fact that her hearers see her in a woman's body, and that means being heard differently, it is the sermon that suffers. Communication is impaired because trying to speak as not a woman, even while obviously being one, poses a barrier to meaning-making. Responding negatively to a woman produces reluctance to listen in some hearers. Women preachers above all have to reject a physical/spiritual dualism in favour of an integrated image of self, because women are seen and heard as women, whether we like it or not. This should impel us along a journey of faith that embodies the emotional, intellectual and spiritual; all experiences of faith, God, sin are valid and worthy of theological reflection.

I did, however, have to address a common conflict for women preachers. How do we intentionally preach as women, while living, learning and working in patriarchal structures? Somehow this must involve challenging the very norms that have produced us – the Church that called us to preach; the Academy that trains us to preach. Challenging male norms can be costly both personally and professionally. We can never see ourselves as others see us, and have no impression of it without talking to them about it. Someone who is balding (male or female) at the back may not find out unless they are told – we can't see the backs of our own heads. Talking about patriarchal culture is a bit like asking what it is like to breathe air. We can't answer the question because we have no alternative with which to compare it.

Finding my own preaching voice meant becoming self-aware. Reflection, as I have said, is essential to the process, the kind of reflection that involves working with others to strive for understanding, not the kind that involves some kind of navel-gazing that yearns after self-realization. Encouragement for anyone, let alone women, to become self-aware is absent both from academic homiletics and practical preaching. When women's preaching is discussed, debate focuses around whether or not we should, rather than what we might bring to the proclamation of the word of God. Realizing our own embodiment, the fact that we experience and understand life through our bodies as well as mind and emotion, brings into relief both how I comprehend life and faith, and how I am seen as preacher and teacher.

Thinking about embodiment led me to explore Bible passages from the perspective of lived experience, drawing parallels with the lived experience of the text. At the same time, it enabled me to think about how I might be seen by the congregation. This was challenging in some respects, for the sermon I shared in the introduction highlighted my impression that I might have been ignored because of my identity as a grandparent, risking my hearers ignoring me for the same reason, perhaps! In this snippet, it is the fact that I am a grandmother that led to some new (to me) thoughts about the Magi's visit to Jesus:

Sermon snippet 1

Leaving alone the stories that have grown up around this scene, and the carol that seems to place these wise people at the manger, the fact that Herod orders boys under the age of two to be killed seems to suggest Jesus was a toddler by this point. These folk from the East arrive not at the cotside of a newborn, but in the home of a toddler. Thinking about this as we spent time with our 18-month-old grandson over Christmas, I wondered whether the early Church that was accused of turning the world upside down was simply emulating the example of the toddler Christ. I wonder what happened on this visit. Perhaps Jesus the toddler climbed on the box of frankincense to get something down off the shelf.

Self

I decided to value and work with my experience as offering a particular, distinctive vantage point when it came to preaching. This meant consciously exploring how my experience affected my Bible reading and my preparation to preach. The next sermon snippet is an example of experience questioning tradition. I had been given two readings on which to base my sermon. Psalm 91 and Matthew 14.22–36. The church leader provided a 'sermon brief' advising me of what they would like me to say. As it turned out, the leader was about to leave, and wanted me to encourage the small, elderly and struggling congregation to step up to the mark and keep the church going. Bearing in mind both my own experience of one of the readings and the situation of my hearers, this is some of what I said:

Sermon snippet 2

I have to admit that I am a bit allergic to the psalm we had read. When our daughter was lying very ill in intensive care somebody recommended that I read it to her. She and I both found it profoundly unhelpful – here we were being encouraged to believe that we would not fear the terror of the night, that we need not fear pestilence and that God would give his people long life, when it was acutely plain that the coming night would be very testing, that the pestilence was rendering my daughter's body helpless and that not only might life not be long but that it was possibly not going to outlast the week.

Psalm 91 had been presented to me, both at the time I describe and when it had been given to me as a preaching text (along with the 'sermon brief'), as a triumphalist song of reassurance. Everything was going to work out as God intended, and we should not worry. The experience of having the psalm quoted in such a way to me in a time of crisis was, as I said, 'profoundly unhelpful'. I therefore decided that I could not, with integrity, use it in the same way with a struggling congregation. My own experience invalidated what I was being encouraged to preach.

Integrity as a teacher meant adjusting my homiletics classes to encourage students' own awareness of self in their preaching, a discomforting process. Attempts to include the person of the preacher in sermon classes seemed dissonant for two reasons: key texts on homiletics have traditionally avoided discussion of the preacher as anything other than a conduit who should remain invisible; imbibing this kind of theology, many seem to regard their own absence from the sermon as 'holy'. Following the unstructured development of my own thinking about self I introduced theological reflection as a method of sermon preparation, perhaps posing a simple question to evoke a shared experience. Just before Advent one year, when the reading for one Sunday was to be Luke 7.18–30, the story of John the Baptist sending to ask Jesus, 'Are you the one who is to come, or are we to wait for another?' (v. 20), a colleague and I began a homiletics session without referencing the text but by asking the question, 'How do you know it's the one?' This generated some very personal reflections in some students, leading to new insight into the text. For me, the exercise meant thinking about the question asked by John in a more down-to-earth way than I had previously. This is the beginning of that sermon:

Sermon snippet 3

'Is this the one?'

I guess you, like me, have spent quite a bit of time on that kind of question in recent weeks. 'Is this the one?'

We're encouraged to ask it at this time of year.

In recent weeks I've spent quite a lot of time asking a similar question, 'Is this the one?' I've done my research, I've talked to other people, I've read about it, I've thought about it. It has occupied quite a bit of my time. And yes, I am pretty confident that I have chosen the right Lego for my grandson's Christmas present.

But I won't know – I won't really know – until it comes to Christmas Day and he unwraps it and I see his face. And of course I will know then, because six-year-olds aren't great at hiding their emotions. Last year when he was five I got a little lecture from him on how grandmas shouldn't really buy grandsons pyjamas for Christmas. I will know. But I don't know yet.

Voice

'Voice' is a major theme both in homiletics and in feminist theology. I have already spoken of it in this chapter. In exegesis we look for the voice of the writer; in homiletics we consider the voice our key instrument; in feminist theology we consider how women's stories have been made unspeakable, how our voice has been suppressed. Nelle Morton spoke of hearing others into speech, Gayatri Chakravorty Spivak talked of speaking for the silenced. Women share experience of living in a world where violence against us has reached pandemic proportions (Storkey, 2015), which might engender a 'common language' that transcends difference. Gender-based violence is the 'great unfinished business of our time' (Alyse Nelson, Vital Voices Global Partnership, cited in Storkey, 2015). 'It's easy to see the strong, set lines of patriarchy in the public face of the Church. Centuries of male popes, patriarchs, cardinals, archbishops, priests, clergy, elders, overseers and theologians have led the flock, exegeted the Scriptures, written the agendas and preached the sermons' (Storkey, 2015: 4). It is time to hear other voices, the other half of the story of faith. Personally, I do not seek to speak for all women, nor to only speak from my own experience, thus avoiding both generalization and essentialism. Rather I try to speak from a recognizably women's perspective and give voice to individual women too, particularly biblical women. Most importantly for my own practice within homiletics, I am finding ways of speaking for myself and of myself for others.

I defined preaching, above, as engaging the people of God in their shared story. My experience of the Women's Voices conference is that there is among women preachers a communality based on living and working in the same kind of environment. For many of us there is also a commitment to telling the truth and a determination to welcome others into community.

When I was asked to preach one Easter Day from John 20.1–18, I wanted to tell Mary's story, give voice, somehow, to her meeting with the risen Jesus.

Sermon snippet 4

'It is finished.' That's what Jesus had said just two days ago. 'It is finished.' His life was finished. His work was finished. His mission to the world, to break through human hardness, human pride, human insistence on religion that had little to do with God. 'It is finished.'

And it was. Finished. The expert executioners had already beaten him. They knew, from years of experience, when a person was dead. And this one was definitely finished.

And so, when Mary went to the tomb two days later she went without hope. She went to tend a dead friend. To do the very last thing she could do for the dead one she had followed.

He was gone. Perhaps she began to realize that although to Jesus she was someone, a person worth listening to, a person to walk with, that too was finished. She was once again the woman from whom demons had been cast out. The woman who down through history was to be remembered as of ill-repute rather than a woman of courageous faith.

In this sermon I was keen to discuss the death and resurrection of Jesus not in rationalist or triumphalist, or even theological terms, but as an event that changed the experience of a woman who had been close to him. I wanted to move the congregation from observers on the sidelines to participants in the story. Moreover, I was keen, having discovered that many preachers regard the Gospel reading of the day almost incidental at Easter time, to preach the text.

Prepared to preach?

Reflecting theologically on my experience of preaching, the culture and tradition within which I have developed, has had prophetic potential. It has both disquieted me and challenged me. I have had to become aware, as do most preachers, of my 'power' role, but also of my subaltern role as a woman whose views are dismissable on the basis of gender. I have moved from being a woman privileged with a voice, seeking to speak on behalf of silenced others, to being more conscious of my own silencing. I am now absolutely convinced of the value of including myself in my preaching, of preaching like a woman. I realized that in preaching that takes testimony seriously the preacher has to develop the spiritual discipline of noticing, the sensitivity to see God at work in the everyday.

In an attempt to develop this discipline, one Lent I decided that rather than give up something, I would take up something. I committed to taking a photograph everyday of something that spoke to me. Some of the results were poor, but one stands out. As I walked early one morning along the side of my local lake, I heard a flock of geese behind me, heading towards me. Camera in hand, finger on button, listening intently, I knew, even felt, the moment when the geese flew over my head. My repeated clicking resulted in an excellent shot of geese in flight, that I was very pleased with. My aim that Lent had been to learn to notice, and the photograph represents what can be achieved if we notice without our eyes. That's the kind of noticing preachers need to develop.

We need to notice where God is at work, yes. We need to notice what is good and holy. But we also need to notice what is wrong – and tell the truth about it. As women we need to notice what happens to us as we experience life through our bodies, as well as in our minds and hearts.

The basic method of preparing to preach that I now teach students, particularly if they are new to preaching or early in their training, starts with 'me'. It encourages the preacher to notice what has been happening to them this week, or when they read the Bible passage, or whatever it might be.

This is the method in brief. It is a step-by-step approach to a more flexible model that we will come to in Chapter 7.

Step	Preparatory task
Step 1	**Experience and Position** (Tradition and Culture) Who am I? Where am I? What have I noticed recently? What do I notice in this Bible passage? How do I feel? This stage often highlights contradictions between what the passage appears to say and my own experience or theology. I usually jot down the questions that it raises for me.
Step 2	**Emerging Themes** What ideas are emerging? Is there something I need to deal with? What is 'fallen' or corrupted here? Where is hope here? What do I believe about them? This stage allows me to focus on one theme, and prevents my mind from going down a path well trodden by others, but of which I have no experience personally.
Step 3	**Research** This is the stage where theological reflection might come in. What do Culture and Tradition say about my theme? How do I answer the questions raised? Now I turn to commentaries to check that the answers I have proposed might be right.
Step 4	**Reflection: Live with it** Can I imagine myself saying *this* to *these* people on *this* day? At this stage I might notice the discomfort of inauthenticity if I try to preach something that sounds right but doesn't match my own experience or position.

Step 5	**Communication**
	How long do I have?
	How will I say what I have decided to say?
	How might it be heard?
	Is anyone excluded?
	I try to emphasize resonance over relevance, and ensure there are ways into the sermon for my hearers.
Step 6	**Final check**
	Has anything happened to change what I am going to say?

Step 1 not only avoids repetition of traditionally accepted interpretations of a Scripture reading, it also ensures that if 'I' am in the sermon, it is as authentic an 'I' as possible. Theological reflection continues throughout the process, and may need more time at one stage than at others, depending on the sermon.

Time for reflection

This reflection is based on 'Preaching as Myself', and is a way of exploring your 'self'.

Who am I?

1.
    At last the secret is out,
    as it always must come in the end,
    (W. H. Auden, 1994, 'At last the secret is out')

As W. H. Auden wrote in his poem of the same name, the fear of many a preacher must be that the secret might come out. The secret that we are not *quite* who we hope our hearers will imagine

---

us to be. The secret that the person we present in the pulpit is not the only person inhabiting the body the congregation sees before it. My realization, and subsequent admission in Snippet 1, that people do see me as someone old enough to be a grandmother, freed me to speak of being ignored because of age. But there are other ways in which we hope not to be seen.

You may have done a Myers–Briggs indicator or an Enneagram at some stage, prompting greater self-knowledge in one way or another. Both, and any other personality indicator tool as well, are rooted in the belief that subconsciously there is more to us than meets the eye. Perhaps we shape ourselves, and are shaped, to fit in. As children we want to please others – parents, teachers, peer group. Certain behaviours are affirmed and reinforced by approval, and so we continue to project the kind of person others seem to want us to be. In her book *Women's Voices* (2017), Nancy Lammers Gross explores ways in which women preachers struggle because they feel a lack of permission to speak. She relates the story of 'Cathy', someone who produced a 'masterful' written sermon on Job, pain and suffering, yet delivered it with a smile on her face. She had been trained to smile in order to make others feel good, and this translated into smiling in the pulpit – no matter what the topic of the sermon. *Ask someone to video you preaching, and watch it to see what your body says about your preaching.*

2. Rather like politicians or celebrities we develop an image of ourselves that is our shop window, the person we want others to think we are (and increasingly the person we want to see ourselves as). It's what Goffman (1990) calls impression management. We arrange our language, our posture and behaviour in ways that will project the person we want to be. When we do that we put the person we don't like into storage, and become a guarded version of ourselves. When we respond to approval and disapproval in this way, we push more and more aspects of ourselves into the store cupboard and try harder and harder to construct the person people like. We might hide things we've done, because of guilt, or things we are because of shame. The more we feel aspects of ourselves are unacceptable, the more prone we might be to depression or outbursts of anger. Telling the truth about ourselves

is an important element of Bible reading, and of authentic preaching. Some truths are hard to tell, even to ourselves. I needed to realize that I too am subaltern. I am not researching and working in the area of women's preaching because I can help others, but also because I need the companionship and understanding I am finding. *What image do you try to project to your congregation? What do you try to hide from them? What have been the keys to your own development?*

3. Choose a section from one of your sermons. *What does it say about you? How might you alter it to include a more authentic 'self'?*

Notes

1 'Once in Royal David's City'.

2 First published in *The Preacher* (No. 154), journal of The College of Preachers.

3 TED talks are talks given by influential, expert speakers and can be found at ted.com

4 Eva's Call was a community piece of art based on experiences of ordinand and ordained women within the Cuddesden community and beyond. It gathered together comments made to them as a form of lament. It can be found online at: https://artsrcc.wordpress.com/2018/03/02/evas-call/

3

Silencing Women:
A Silencing Culture

Before we embark on this chapter we need to agree some ground rules. How do we speak of equality, of the oppression of women and of patriarchal systems without appearing to blame men or cast them in the role of villain? Patriarchy is oppressive, and renders women subaltern, without a voice. It does so in science, the arts, politics and religion. But we need to define it carefully before we examine what it does and how it does it.

Patriarchy is not a battle of the sexes, or the oppression of one half of the human race by the other; it damages all of us. It is not a system – systems are easily changed, yet injustices continue even when rules are amended. I want to suggest that patriarchy is a narrative we all live in, and through which we understand life, faith and God. Narratives are powerful, because they pervade everything, and as a result are difficult to spot. In this chapter I want to look at how the patriarchal narrative influences all aspects of our lives, and how we might, as women preachers, tell the truth about it. I want to do this not just for the benefit of women, but for the benefit of those boys and men who want to understand a woman's perspective, and who feel they have been deprived of one half of the Christian story.

I want to start by thinking about Culture. The culture we live in in most of the West, that influences us even in childhood. Our primary schools are full of aspiring inventors, sports people, business leaders and politicians. There seems to be limitless self-belief and no concept of odds that might be stacked against anyone.

Then something terrible happens. Some children learn the word 'no'. Not the no of a loving parent introducing boundaries and keeping their kids from eating too many sweets or not sleeping enough or running out near roads or walking too close to a fire. But the harsh, horrible no of 'know your place'. The no that, for some of us, gets more and more deafening with age, but which seems – like a dog whistle – to be completely inaudible to others who don't simply fail to respond; they don't even know it's there.

It's the no that says skipping ropes are for girls and science kits are for boys. It's the no that says nice girls don't and plain ones better watch out in case they get left on the shelf. The no that says it doesn't matter whether you've a Cambridge professorship, an OBE or your own BBC series: you're still just an object to be appraised by cyber judges more interested in your body than your brain.

The most dangerous effect of that 'no' is that it gets so deeply internalized you start saying it silently to yourself. You get so used to extra hurdles being put in your way that it becomes too exhausting to even think about clearing them – and then you forget you even can clear them. (Sarah Brown in Laura Bates, 2014: 5).

Culture

At around the time women across the world were beginning to protest their right to be treated equally, Scottish philosopher Thomas Carlyle said this: 'The history of the world is but the biography of great men.'

I rather suspect he was right. At least, history *insofar as it is told*, is but the biography of great men. Sadly, just as we remembered, until the recent film (*Hidden Figures*), that John Glenn was the first man to orbit the earth, we forgot that the mathematical genius of Mary Jackson made it possible. No doubt we remember something of Martin Luther King's 'I have a dream' speech, but forget that it was Mahalia Jackson, standing behind him that day in August 1963, who told him to 'tell them about the dream'. There has been no shortage of brave, powerful, influential women in the arts, sciences or theology. The problem is that her-story is rarely told. A male perspective has dominated, airbrushing women out.

Media

Let's look at how women are treated in some key areas of modern culture, beginning with media.

Much of the world is media rich, even swamped. Editors and journalists interject up-to-date information into our days at regular intervals, unless, of course, we set our phones and tablets and computers not to receive news bulletins. Ostensibly, we are always in touch. But there are other more sinister messages hidden in the way women and men are reported in the media. Women's words are usually summarized, where men are often quoted verbatim. Women leaders are presented as bodies, sex objects, convenient and appropriate targets of men's judgement. Take, for example, the way some newspapers wrote of Prime Minister Theresa May and First Minister of Scotland Nicola Sturgeon. Their meeting in 2016 was not reported by the *Sun* newspaper as a discussion about political difference, the future of their two countries, or the recent Brexit referendum. No. The focus was on shoes. Was Nicola Sturgeon trying to present Scotland's case, or negotiate for her country? No. She was trying to 'out-shoe' Theresa May.

Thank God for the SNP's economics adviser Miriam Brett, who responded to the *Sun*'s online Twitter news with the comment, 'You spelled "First Minister of Scotland negotiates economic and trade strategy with the Prime Minister" wrong.'

The following year, as Brexit became the only real news item in most papers, the *Daily Mail* dealt with a similar meeting between the two with similar deference. 'Never mind Brexit,' declared its headline writer, 'who won legs-it?' Two influential and capable women were thereby objectivized for the benefit of misogynist readers.

Even at thoughtful, Christian festivals like Greenbelt the same attitude is expressed thoughtlessly by some. Amal Alamuddin is a human rights lawyer. Among others she has represented a journalist wrongly detained in Egypt, a Libyan prosecuted in the International Criminal Court, and the Kingdom of Cambodia before the International Court of Justice. She is visiting professor at Columbia Law School where she teaches Human Rights. She was an adviser to Kofi Annan when he was the UN Envoy on Syria. She is a human rights lawyer with a great track record. Yet, a journalist given the stage at the Greenbelt Festival in 2017 suggested that publishing photographs of her revealing an expanse of leg, as she got out of a car, was a reasonable way of bringing her human rights work to public attention. It was a price she should be willing to pay. Apparently for a woman to gain attention she needs to be portrayed in ways prescribed by a patriarchal media.

Press handling of a tragic murder–suicide in 2016 will illustrate the way women are masked out of events. A father stabbed to death his wife and three children before turning the knife on himself. He was variously described as honourable, a valued community member, committed and normal. His mental illness prompted calls for better funding of mental health services. Headlines focused quickly on the children: 'How could he kill those poor boys?'; 'Wonderful children who will be missed by all who knew them'; 'Killed in their pyjamas by father in frenzied attack – before mother-in-law found note'. Journalists dug into the man's past even further over the coming days: 'Quiet and a real gentleman'; 'The sole person who would do anything for anybody at any time of day or night'; 'Very obliging'. A decent man had killed his family because he was mentally ill. It was, of course, a tragedy. This man, given such sensitive treatment in the press, had murdered his children 'in their pyjamas'. He had also killed his wife. What happened to her in the coverage? 'Rest in peace, invisible mother,' wrote Linnea Dunne in *The Guardian* (31 August 2016). It is illustrative of the way in which women either disappear or are objectified in the media. Importantly, it is the way the world is portrayed by and to our congregations.

I don't believe that many journalists or editors set out to denigrate women. I think it more likely that they tell us the story we understand, the patriarchal narrative that silences women. Unchallenged, the narrative becomes all-pervasive.

Science

Let's look at some examples from other aspects of life. Darwinian evolution is embraced by many who see the damage done by the Genesis account of creation to the rights of women. Evolutionary science affects how we human beings understand ourselves, how children are taught, how religion is critiqued. So let's go back to its founder – Charles Darwin. 'I certainly think that women ... are inferior intellectually,' he wrote, 'and it seems to me to be a great difficulty from the laws of inheritance ... in their becoming the intellectual equals of men.'[1] A friend of Darwin, George Romanes, further insisted that 'from her abiding sense of weakness and consequent dependence, there also arises in woman that deeply-rooted desire to please the opposite sex which, beginning in the terror of a slave, has ended in the devotion of a wife' (Romanes, 1887: 383–401; Saini, 2018: 392). Quaint as this might sound, the reasoning parallels quite a bit of thinking in the contemporary Church about the role of women.

It is redundant here to point out the wide-ranging influence of Darwinian ideas. An important question to ponder, though, is to what extent the culture in which Darwin lived affected his theories, as well as how his theories influenced subsequent culture. As Simone de Beauvoir said, 'To prove women's inferiority, antifeminists began to draw not only, as before, on religion, philosophy and theology, but also on science'

(2010: 12). Certainly, the idea that males and females evolved at different rates and in different ways has engendered a host of studies. The interpretation of results, however, has always been swayed by cultural expectation. Take as an example the idea that women talk more than men. It is widely accepted – check out comments over after-service coffee in church! Lise Elliot, associate professor of neuroscience at Rosalind Franklin University, analysed data from a large number of studies in which neurological differences between men and women were claimed. 'Sex differences in the brain are irresistible to those looking to explain stereotypic differences,' she says. Such studies 'often make a bigger splash, in spite of being based on small samples. But as we explore multiple datasets and are able to coalesce very large samples of males and females, we find these differences often disappear or are trivial' (cited in Saini, 2018: 112). In other words, if you are looking for something you will find it.

Why is this important to women preachers? 'Because what science tells us about women profoundly shapes how society thinks about the sexes' (Saini, 2018). Our interpretations of biblical stories are freighted with meaning from our own culture. That culture is shaped by the patriarchal narrative, supported by apparently objective scientific endeavour, that women are different from men, and in many ways inferior to them. When we come to preaching, part of our responsibility is to examine our underlying assumptions and inspect the narratives that support them. We will explore later the ways in which these narratives affect our readings of some biblical women.

Arts

Let's turn to look at the arts, to see whether they fare better than the media or science.

On International Women's Day, 2017, Mendelssohn's Easter Sonata was given a belated premier. It was performed for the first time under the name of its actual composer, Fanny Mendelssohn. The piece had been lost for 150 years and when found was attributed to her more famous brother, Felix. How was it that the composer was misidentified? Although brother and sister were equally gifted, their father decided that for a girl, music could only ever be a pleasant pastime. Apparently, Felix thought he was doing Fanny a favour by publishing her work under his name.

This isn't a unique story. Clara Schumann is best known, because of something she said, as the wife of composer Robert: 'I once believed ... that I possessed creative talent, but I have given up the idea. A woman must not desire to compose.' Her father had been fanatically ambitious and drove her musical ability hard, having her perform publicly from a young age. She started writing her Piano Concerto Opus 7 at the age of 13 and first performed it at the age of 16. She met the promiscuous Robert Schumann in 1828, and Robert seems to have proposed marriage on the advice of his doctor. At the time, he had syphilis, contracted from one of his sexual liaisons. His physician told him that a wife would cure him. Despite his promises that Clara could remain active as an artist, Robert later wrote, 'Clara herself knows her main occupation is as a mother and is happy in the circumstances and would not want them changed.'

In these stories women's talents are almost casually sacrificed to men's. It is still part of the accepted narrative in many quarters, and affects our presentation of many Bible women. Sarai is one example. In Genesis 12 Abram is in Egypt. He fears that Pharaoh will want to take Sarai for himself because she is beautiful. Taking trouble to explain how this might be her fault, Abram says, 'I know well that you are a woman beautiful in appearance; and when the Egyptians see you, they will say, "This is his wife"; then they will kill me, but they will let you live. Say you are my sister, so that it may go well with me because of you, and that my life may be spared on your account' (vv. 11–13). 'From the moment Abram decides he will not choose to stand his ground as her husband, Sarai's fate is decided: she will be "taken" by another man' (Williams,

2014: 39). She will be taken either because she follows Abram's plan or because she does not, in which case she will become a widow, and again be taken by Pharaoh. Sarai's choice can affect only what happens to her husband. Her fate is sealed by his cowardice.

Examples like Fanny Mendelssohn and Clara Schumann grate with us today. Yet even in the twenty-first century, women are treated as inferior in aspects of art. The Bechdel test, developed in 1985, is a simple way of assessing the role of women in films. To pass it, a film must have a conversation between two named women about something other than men. Around half of all films pass it. Among the top 100 American films of 2011, women accounted for 33 per cent of all characters and 11 per cent of protagonists. Expectations in the movies seem to be that men lead and women follow, and that women find it tricky to speak about things other than men. I wonder what the outcomes would be if preachers were to apply a 'sermon Bechdel test' to what we say. Certainly, in my early days of preaching, my focus would be on active men and passive women, and my exegeses would be from a male perspective. Probably at one time I praised Mary of Bethany for her passive sitting at Jesus' feet, and condemned her sister Martha for not dropping everything to listen to the Lord. Now I would praise Mary for sitting in the space normally occupied by a man, and remind my hearers that Martha's organizational abilities were most likely of great value in the early Church!

In summer 2018 I visited the Island of Bute. Coincidentally we arrived on the weekend of Bute Noir, a crime writers' festival. Thanks to my husband's remarkable persistence, I managed to get a ticket for the discussion on violence against women in crime fiction. It was revelatory, and mirrors, in many ways, the dilemma of women preachers in contemporary society.

Four accomplished women authors formed the panel, each speaking first about their own work. One spoke of writing a scene of violence against a woman. She was struggling. The scene didn't feel right. At some point she came to the realization that she had been writing it from a 'male' perspective. Once she began to rewrite it from the woman's viewpoint the story flowed. One of the panellists said something along these lines: 'It's our responsibility as women writers to tell women's stories. If we don't, who will?' As a woman preacher, the comment resonated.

Discussion turned to a new literary award, the Staunch Book Award. It was to be (and has since been) awarded to 'the author of a novel in the thriller genre in which no woman is beaten, stalked, sexually exploited, raped or murdered'. Was this a good thing? Initially, it sounded as though it might be. But then woman after woman made the point that if violence against us is not written about, it will be airbrushed out. How we as preachers handle the things people don't want to hear about is a vitally important question.

Partway through the discussion about women's crime fiction, discussion about women in crime writing was brought to a halt by a seemingly innocuous question: 'What about the men?' The speaker went on to point out that men too suffer violence, and that not all are bad. Nobody disagreed. The question framed the discussion about women's experiences as binary. Saying that bad things happened to women was somehow restructured to imply bad things don't happen to men. Patriarchal narrative asserts itself by devaluing discussion that challenges it. It does so by removing any difference between women's and men's experiences.

This has been a brief, idiosyncratic roam through areas of culture that affect, and reflect, our thinking. They illustrate the thought-world our congregations, and we, inhabit. They matter, because they affirm the patriarchal narrative and enable it to be handed down to the next generation. So-called 'parenting guru' Steve Biddulph wrote in *Raising Boys* (2015): 'In an anti-male era, it's important to remember that men built the planes, fought the wars, laid the railroad tracks, invented the cars, built the hospitals, invented the medicines and sailed the ships that made it all happen' (cited by Jenni Murray, 2016, to which she replied, 'Rubbish!'). Clearly, people like Rosalind Franklin, the biophysicist whose work ultimately led to the discovery of the DNA helix; Lise Meitner, a nuclear physicist, a key member of the group that worked on nuclear fission; Melissa Franklin, a particle physicist, whose work led to the discover of quarks; and Chien Shiung Wu, whose work led to the separation of uranium, had slipped his mind. To say nothing of such a well-known figure as Marie Curie, whose work with radium led to both X-rays and the splitting of the atom. She was the first women to gain a PhD in France, and the first woman to win the Nobel Prize. At her award ceremony the President of the Swedish Academy included in his speech words from the Bible: 'It is not good that a man should be alone, I will make a helpmeet for him.'

Tradition

The email pinged into my inbox sooner than I expected. A response to my application. A colleague had recommended me as chaplain for occasional weeks with a Christian holiday company. I had written, explaining how I was qualified for such a role, including the fact that I had holidayed with the company several years running. The reply was blunt – so blunt, in fact, that I did not at first understand it: 'Dear Liz, as you will understand there are complementarians and egalitarians. Were your husband to apply to be chaplain and you to be his helper, I'm sure we would accept.'

How did we get to this, in the Church?

A brief history

Many discussions about women's preaching begin with the assumption that it is a new thing – the Church needs to keep up with the times, and so on. Opponents cite Scripture, firing out-of-context verses randomly at 'egalitarians'. Yet the pertinent question is surely not whether women should be included in preaching, but when and how they were excluded from it?

We have no texts of early sermons, although the Acts of the Apostles gives us some clues as to what Paul might have said. Paul used testimony. He told his story three times in Acts (chapters 9, 22, 26). He was culturally relevant, finding God around him (14) – he realized the value of 'noticing'. He used persuasion (28) and he engaged political power (25). Other than that, we know nothing about the content of very early preaching. We know that the message of Jesus' resurrection was entrusted to women: 'go and tell my brothers' (Matthew 28.10); 'go, tell his disciples and Peter' (Mark 16.7); 'Remember how he told you ... Then they remembered his words, and ... they told all this to the eleven and to all the rest' (Luke 24.6–8); 'But go to my brothers and say' (John 20.17). We know that Paul did not sanction exclusion on the grounds of race, class or gender (Gal. 3.27–28). In his liturgical instructions to the church in Corinth, Paul details how and when women should speak: 'any woman who prays or prophesies' (1 Cor. 11.5). There is no prohibition on women's speaking, they are simply asked to observe decorum that would commend them to the culture round about. The discussion in Paul's letter to the Corinthians is of particular interest to contemporary women preachers. It contains some of the verses presented as biblical injunctions to our silencing. It also illustrates how debates between church and surrounding culture proceed. In first-century Corinth women were enjoying greater equality. No doubt Corinthian Christian women expected to find their new freedoms in the church. Paul, on the other hand, was an old-school Pharisee. He had been raised with a patriarchal narrative – he was a Roman citizen, structure and hierarchy were important; he was a Pharisee, keen on racial purity. Perhaps there was more than theological concern alone behind Paul's instruction. Given that we have only one half of the conversation, it is impossible to put the whole into a context, but I wonder whether we take seriously enough Paul's call, to both his sisters and brothers, to be mature in thinking: 'Brothers and sisters, do not be children in your thinking ... in thinking be adults (1 Cor. 14.20).

Despite this, by the time the second letter to Timothy was written (at least 60 years after Paul's death), an imperative against women's leadership had crystallized. Canonization of the New Testament worked against women, for it came at a time when they had no voice; they were trapped in a vicious circle. Those with ecclesial authority decided what was included in the Canon; books chosen for inclusion were deemed to transmit 'divine revelation'; the interpretation of these books determined theological 'truth'; this 'truth' determined who had authority. Unsurprisingly, it was not long before gatherings that allowed women to serve at the altar were censured by church authorities, and by the fifth century every expression of the Christian faith that upheld the authority of women to preach, teach or lead had been opposed by the institutional Church (King, 1998: 29).

One of the effects was that women's voices were lost. Those who wanted to be heard had first to subjugate their identity as women. Thus Hildegard of Bingen prefaced her writings with, 'I am but a poor creature and fragile vessel' (Bowie, 1990: 130). In the English church this subjugation came earlier. In 664 Hilda, Abbess of Whitby, hosted a contentious synod whose aim was to define the dating of Easter. Hilda was an outstanding leader and gifted teacher. Five of her students became bishops. One of them, Wilfred, was very impressed by the pomp and ceremony of the church in Rome when he visited, and he was sent back to England to tame the Celtic church that defended equality, community and poverty. Imagine Hilda's pain when she saw Wilfred forsake what she had taught him and argue for the might of Rome. Basically, the controversy was not about dates, but about power.

Where are we now?

For centuries the Church has used gender as an organizing category to suppress women's voices. It adopted contemporary values not deliberately, but because they fitted the prevailing narrative. We live in different times, and despite identifiable traces of this same narrative across the whole of our society, questions are being asked of it. We have preaching women, and much has been written about how we do it and how we are heard. Despite that, little has been written about the prophetic potential of women's proclamation. Opportunities for women can be inferred from the work of key homileticians: Craddock insists that 'one cannot separate what one hears in a sermon from the one who delivers it' (1985: 84), for example, though he does not make apparent women's distinctive contribution to the enterprise. Similarly, Buttrick (1987) points to 'orientation' as essential to preaching, but does not deal with orientation of gender. Long, a third primary source for homiletic thought, also fails to explore how gospel proclamation is enriched and expanded by preaching women.

Little work has been done to ascertain the effectiveness of preaching. Most writing is done by homileticians and is therefore based on the assumption that, one way or another, a sermon is a worthwhile endeavour. In what way is assessed largely according to the preaching models we saw earlier. Effectiveness for those who embrace the 'preacher as instructor' model consists of having said something. For 'pastor preachers' it lies in having something heard. A micro-survey conducted in 2009 in England suggested that while 63.7 per cent of churchgoers look forward to the sermon 'frequently', and 33.2 per cent do so 'sometimes', only 17 per cent said that sermons changed how they lived.[2] Apparently we are rather more successful at speaking than being heard. Maybe it is because we preach out of context, failing to recognize the culture and tradition in which we live, and that influences our hearers' understanding. Miscommunication transpires when the preacher seems to speak from a world unknown to the hearers, and when the everyday lives of hearers appear foreign to the speaker. This is key to women's preaching. It is by noticing the presence of God in the everyday experience of women that women's faith-lives become speakable. A task of women preachers is surely to speak of faith, life and God based not on biological sex or gender, but on the basis of shared experience of patriarchal culture and history.

Where are we now? Women are preaching in many branches of the Church. Women's preaching is being written about, but its distinctive prophetic possibilities are largely ignored, and women are being invited into the existing company of preachers, rather than being asked to help redefine preaching itself.

Telling the truth about patriarchy and sexism

This is where I think we are in terms of our culture and our tradition. It has not been good news for women or for women preachers. As Gloria Steinem, a prominent feminist in the 1960s and 1970s said: 'The truth will set you free, but first it will p*** you off.'

Being p****d off is not enough, however. As women preachers our task is to declare, with Mary, that

> God has brought down the powerful from their thrones,
>   and lifted up the lowly;
> God has filled the hungry with good things,
>   and sent the rich away empty.
> God has helped God's people,
>   in remembrance of mercy,
> according to the covenant with our ancestors,
>   to Sarah and Rachel and Rebekah and Ruth.
>   (My translation)

St Augustine told a short but encouraging story: 'Hope has two beautiful daughters. Their names are Anger and Courage. Anger at the way things are, and courage to do something about it.' It's fine to be angry about the dominant patriarchal narrative, and we must remember that in following the example of Jesus, turning over tables and chasing people out is an option. But being angry is not enough. We also need the courage to do something about it. That's at least one of the things to be learned from the recent centenary celebration of partial women's suffrage. Without courage the women we remember, Emmeline Pankhurst, Christabel Pankhurst, Annie Kenney, Emily Davison, Muriel Matters and others, would have achieved nothing. The same is true of those women, and those men, who prayed and argued and fought for the ordination of women.

Anger and courage are essential if there is to be hope, but I think there is a third ingredient – persistence. If we are to take seriously the call to preach as women, we need to preach not only from the front of church, but in the way that we live each day, and the way we notice what is going on around us. The patriarchal narrative that renders women's lives and faith inconsequential grows in the fertile soil of simple, thoughtless, everyday acts of sexism. Sexism is different from patriarchy. We all live in a patriarchal society that damages both men and women. We are not all sexist, however. Sexism is a choice, conscious or unconscious, and it can be stopped.

What is sexism?

Sexism is so pervasive it easily goes unnoticed. Often, it is not even intentional. When, for example, managers of the Barbican theatre in London decided to make their toilets gender neutral it was, in their words, in order to provide 'a supportive, inclusive and flexible space for all our audiences and staff'. The effect, however, was that women had to queue even longer, because while men could use what were formerly women's toilets, women could not use the formerly men's ones, because they still had urinals. What was intended for good was, in fact, detrimental, simply because nobody asked how the change would affect women.

Sexism is historic. It underpinned social structures and church teaching during the 1950s and early 1960s, an era to which many congregation members look back nostalgically. 'A social service meeting, an afternoon tea, a matinee, a whatnot, is no excuse for there being no dinner ready when a husband comes home from a hard day's work' (Revd Alfred Henry Tyrer, 1951 cited in Oneill, 2013). For some of our congregations, preaching a good sermon is no excuse for not have dinner ready either!

Sexism is accepted. Assumptions that gender injustice is 'just how things are' is also sexism, including assumptions that women clergy are better suited to teaching Sunday school than are men, or that men are better preachers. A congregation member once told me, 'You were so good I forgot you are a woman.' I still don't know how I should have responded.

Sexism is both hostile and benevolent (Glick and Fiske, 2001: 109). Hostile sexism is 'antipathy toward women who are viewed as usurping men's power'. The online respondent to my article on women's preaching voices, who claimed this was 'the sort of unequal thinking rife in the world of feminism', demonstrated hostile sexism. Benevolent sexism enacts 'a subjectively favourable, chivalrous ideology that offers protection and affection to women who embrace conventional roles'. It 'pacifies women's resistance' because it 'sounds so darn friendly'. Typically it might be exposed in comments such as 'I don't know why you women want equality. You're much better than me', or in a protective arm around the shoulder.

Sexism is found in small acts of everyday communication; microaggressions that undermine us because we are women. One example might be blaming a woman's anger on being hormonal, even when she has something to be angry about; another is the assumption that women can't park or read maps – or, indeed, that men are proud and won't ask directions. Another is 'mansplaining', which seems to affect women preachers and teachers particularly. It is the act of talking condescendingly to someone (usually a woman), about something of which the (male) speaker has incomplete knowledge.

Until recently, sexism has been a bit like climate change. 'Human beings tend to cling to convenient obliviousness – "I haven't seen it, so it can't really exist!" – in spite of embarrassing, burgeoning bodies of evidence to the contrary' (Bates, 2014: 24). So how do we undermine its power?

First, by telling the truth about it. That takes courage. In her excellent book, *SHE*, Karoline Lewis (2016: 169) says:

> We do not speak up because we do not believe anyone will listen, or that anything will change. So we stay silent: for ourselves, for others, in shame, in guilt, hoping that someone else will say something, speak up, stand for justice, work against discrimination, reject false claims about God, and free us from theologies that judge. We hope that someone else will speak up for those abused, for those who have no voice. We hope that someone else will give voice to what we feel and know and want, that someone else will speak up for us.

Maybe someone else will. But if you are in the pulpit that day, maybe you are meant to be that someone else for your congregation.

We cannot denounce the ill-treatment of girls around the world, through FGM or prostitution or low wage or anything else, if we tolerate actions and attitudes that marginalize them in our own congregations. We cannot denounce the ill-treatment of women around the world if we preach from a Bible that treats them as sources of temptation and sin. We have to speak the truth persistently about sexism in the world, in the Church and in the Bible.

I am not convinced that we have a gospel to proclaim if the gospel we proclaim does not require gender equality. I don't accept that there can be good news for some but not others, or that good news for some is more important than good news for all.

Standing in a queue waiting to get into a comedy musical at the Edinburgh Fringe, my husband and I overheard a fascinating conversation. Two of the people involved had, at one time, apparently, been committed members of a well-known Anglican church somewhere in the south of England. But they had stopped attending, and their companions were intrigued as to the reason. 'The thing is,' said the woman, 'they said everyone was welcome, but what they really meant was that men were welcome to become leaders of things, and women were welcome to brew up and do the pots.' The tragedy of it was that because this one specific church thought that way, these people assumed the whole Church agreed and did so because it's what the Bible says.

If we, as preachers, are complacent, tolerant or silent about oppressive interpretations of the Bible, we convey to our congregations that such treatment of women is acceptable. Women will assume they have to live with it or leave. Men will assume you don't mind and carry on as before. The script we have been handed by preachers who have preceded us needs some serious revision.

How, then, are we to work with our source script, the Bible?

Hermeneutics and homiletics

All preaching should be biblical preaching, at least as far as I am concerned. The question is what we do with the Bible in our preaching. It is not enough to dismiss it as hopelessly out of date or irredeemably sexist, as some have done. It will not do to accept some bits but not others. Even if we fail to see it, others will surely notice a lack of integrity in a position that encourages us to ignore some biblical texts while taking others at face value. Taking the Bible at face value, we surely conclude that women should neither lead nor preach. Between these two poles, we must, as women preachers, find a coherent, authentic stance about the Bible.

I want to start by looking at some key thinkers, what they have to say about biblical interpretation and where women's Bible reading might fit.

Friedrich Schleiermacher: Christmas Eve: Dialogue on the Incarnation *(1806)*

Schleiermacher presented his account of situated understanding by means of a short story, Christmas Eve. In it a household gathers, having returned from a communion service. The men discuss the rational problems of the incarnation, while the women seem to know the newborn Jesus suprarationally. Leaving aside the essentialism of the story, that men necessarily behave one way and women another, Schleiermacher's point is that too often the Bible had been subjected to 'masculine' analysis, and too seldom to 'feminine' devotional understanding. His thesis was that the two were complementary, so all understanding of Scripture is provisional and incomplete. All biblical interpretation is subject to the experience and belief position of the interpreter. Here is room for women's interpretation of the Bible in the light of women's experiences. Complete understanding, according to Schleiermacher, 'always involves an apparent circle' in which 'each part can be understood only out of the whole to which it belongs, and vice versa'.

Rudolph Bultmann: Is Exegesis without Presuppositions Possible? *(1957, 1965 in English)*

In his classic article Is Exegesis without Presupposition Possible?, Bultmann queried the possibility of exegesis without presupposition when he challenged the kind of Christian faith that developed from Enlightenment thinking, where truth is objectively knowable. His proposal was that understanding history is only possible 'for one who does not stand over against it as a neutral, nonparticipating spectator, but himself [sic] stands in history and shares responsibility for it'. While Karl Barth accused Bultmann of allowing existential philosophy to determine his reading of Scripture, for women exegetes this again offers scope for new work.

Hans Frei: The Eclipse of Biblical Narrative *(1974)*

The development of new approaches to homiletics was preceded by calls for new approaches to hermeneutics. Hans Frei was a significant contributor to this work. The hegemony of historical criticism in biblical study had led to a 'breakdown of realistic and figural interpretation of biblical stories'. The story itself had been lost, he said, through the hermeneutical efforts of those, such as Schleiermacher, who suggested there could be no such thing as exegesis without presupposition, and those who focused on how the position and experience of biblical writers and readers each contributed to biblical interpretation. Using Auerbach's concept of Mimesis, the way in which a writer conveys the sense of a world to the reader, and Barth's theory of God's revelatory narrative, Frei proposed the biblical narrative be approached from a hermeneutic of faith, accepting Bible stories as fundamentally trustworthy.

He wanted to reclaim the narrative of biblical faith by proposing that Bible stories speak truth.

A significant problem with Frei's work was the failure to take account of situated understanding (understanding through experience and position) and his promotion of reading without conceptual baggage. His achievement was to remind theologians that the Bible is narrative and that narrative (and Scripture) is a way of structuring experience.

Both Brueggemann and Frei, in seeking to assert the importance of the biblical text, fail to deal adequately with the problem that it has been interpreted in ways that oppress women. Brueggemann lumps together being white and being male, not in a discussion of Scripture but in an acknowledgement that some might find the challenges of Postmodernism more difficult than others. Neither examines the text of the Bible or the history of its interpretation from an experiential perspective.

Paul Ricoeur: Hermeneutics of Testimony *(1980)*

According to Ricoeur texts have both plot and referent, the plot being internal, the referent external. Each contributes to meaning; neither makes sense without the other. Where Frei's narrative theory requires presuppositionless exegesis, Ricoeur wants to ask of the narrative, 'According to whom is this the plot?' According to Ricoeur the Bible cannot be its own authority, we cannot employ the argument that the Bible is true because it says it is. Christian interpretation is not based in fact, but in testimony – 'this is what I have seen and understood'. In this model testimony is a way of deciding between points of view, and preaching is an attempt to persuade. Ricoeur notices in Isaiah that the person bearing testimony is sent; that their witness is intrinsically global, rather than personal or specific; that they proclaim something for all people; and that their task requires total engagement. Although Ricoeur does not specifically say so, his model of interpretation offers support to the argument that because of what we have seen and heard, women offer a different testimony from men (Brueggemann, 1997).

Based on what we have seen thus far, I want to propose that reclaiming biblical narrative, as Frei suggested, is a worthwhile and important venture for women preachers. That theories of meaning and interpretation, particularly in Schleiermacher and Ricoeur, encourage us to believe that our own experience of faith, life and God provides a valuable tool to mine the Bible's rich seams of truth. I also want to propose that four key sources, used in my preferred model of theological reflection, provide a way for all preachers to critically engage with their text, bearing in mind both their own experience and belief. Exploring texts in this way enables us to acknowledge our presuppositions, and allow them to dialogue with Scripture.

Walter Brueggemann: Cadences of Home: Preaching Among Exiles *(1997)*

It seems virtually impossible to study homiletics nowadays without encountering Walter Brueggemann. He is a prolific writer, but I will contain myself to just two aspects of his work. First, he rightly urges biblical preaching as liberative for an exiled people. We live under a dominant narrative, which he sees as Enlightenment thought, from which the Bible needs to be freed in order to offer a local and specific one. He regards the Bible as 'a set of models (paradigms) of reality made up of images situated in and contextualized by narratives'. Once liberated from manipulation, the text can speak justice by making visible the vulnerable among us.

While all the time claiming that the Bible speaks to the 'exile' in liberative ways, Brueggemann dismisses feminism ('bra burning') as an 'act of defiance against "sacred order"', and essentializes human experience, setting up biblical narrative against his own construction of 'what the baptized know' (144). He concedes the point that dominant theologies have monopolized theological language, rendering others mute and powerless, but suggests that the work of feminist theologians reduces the debate to a dualist dichotomy in which good equals feminist and bad equals patriarchal. Thus he demonstrates his submission to the patriarchal narrative, and is saved the problem of trying to redeem language from the grasp of existing hegemonies. Women's preaching must agree with Brueggemann about preaching among exiles, and seeking freedom from the pathologies of our society – the dominant narrative. However, we must decline to accept that what Brueggemann calls the 'sacred order' is anything other than the patriarchal narrative we would want to question.

Second, and more positively, Brueggemann encourages us to read the language of the Old Testament, and learn to speak it. He has worked with some of Ricoeur's ideas to describe the speech patterns of the Hebrew Bible as testimony, recounting what the people of God have heard and seen. Interpretation of

Scripture should include finding the disruptive prophetic voice and knowing both 'the tradition of wisdom and the dailiness of life'. Recounting what the women of God have heard and seen, and knowing the 'dailiness' of women's lives, will render Scripture liberative in new ways in our preaching.

We move to look briefly at what women theologians have said of the biblical text.

Rosemary Radford Ruether: Sexism and God-Talk: Toward a Feminist Theology *(1983)*

'No new prophetic tradition ever is interpreted in a cultural vacuum,' wrote Ruether, thereby agreeing with both Schleiermacher and Bultmann. Rather than offering an alternative to culture, as Brueggemann suggests, Ruether insists that the Bible has been domesticated by patriarchal culture. Biblical exegesis must seek an alternative tradition, more deeply rooted in Scripture than the one that has been corrupted. Feminist biblical criticism needs to criticize the dominant patriarchal narrative by reaching the deep 'bedrock of authentic Being upon which to ground the self' (15). Five assumptions underpin her approach to biblical exegesis: God's defence and vindication of the oppressed; God's antipathy towards dominant power structures; God's reign of justice and peace, which is to come; a vision of an age to come, in which injustice is overcome and God's reign is realized; dissension from religious ideology. She critiques 'male advocacy of the poor and oppressed', saying, 'liberation must start with the oppressed of the oppressed, namely *women* of the oppressed'.

Taking Old Testament prophetic writing as an example, Ruether explores intersectionality, the way in which various social identities contribute to oppression. The prophets, for example, identified with the rural classes against the oppressively wealthy cities and powerful empires, but failed to recognize 'the oppressiveness of their own rule over wives, daughters, and slaves' (27). In the New Testament Paul argued against ethnocentric religion, but was unable to practise ideas of equality between male and female. Oppressed people are not homogenous groups, nor are they innocent of oppressing others. Rather, relationships are complex. Key to understanding a biblical message that includes the liminal is not regarding past texts as the point of reference, but instead 'the liberated future'. Feminism, according to Ruether, 'presumes a radical concept of "sin"' (135).

'The most basic expression of human community, the I–Thou relation as the relationship of men and women, has been distorted throughout all known history into an oppressive relationship that has victimized one half of the human race and turned the other half into tyrants.' Here, for women preachers, lies not simply a call to 'just preaching' but a call to specific, situated, liberative preaching.

Elizabeth Schüssler Fiorenza: In Memory of Her: A Feminist Theological Reconstruction of Christian Origins (1994)

The Bible story needs to be reconstructed, making room for women, according to Fiorenza. '[T]he Bible often fails to supply women with liberating texts that are readily available for the poor and the sojourner. Rather than emancipating women, the Bible is, quite often, at the root of the problem' (76). She proposes a theological task in which I believe women preachers must engage, the 'reconstruction of early Christian origins in a feminist perspective' (31). This will involve separating 'the liberating Tradition from the androcentric-patriarchal texts of the Bible' (21). We must move from rereading the same meanings into oppressive texts, 'to the construction of a life-centre that generates new cultural texts, traditions and mythologies' (21).

Rebecca Chopp: The Power to Speak: Feminism, Language, God *(2002)*

Chopp offers a clear reason for women to preach as women. Unless our voices help to 'revise the social and symbolic rules of language' that govern who gets to speak and who is heard, women will be 'forever strangers' in the congregation (2). '[T]he simple naming of experiences by women has been the first step toward creating a narrative agency of and by women,' she wrote earlier (1995: 35). Characteristic of a new register for preaching must be the hearing and naming of women's stories, the ability of women to 'construct the ongoing living narratives'.

For Chopp, language is not neutral and knowledge is not abstract. She identifies three ways in which feminist processes can enrich preaching practice and undermine the dominant patriarchal narrative. The first principle is awareness of difference, not a dualistic distinction between all women and all men, but gender difference as a starting point for recognizing other differences. The second principle is recognition. For Chopp, recognition is awareness. We might recognize our condition, and having recognized it see new theological possibilities to explain it. The third principle is a vision for justice. Women preachers speak not simply because they have the opportunity but also the necessary resources.

Susan Durber: Preaching Like a Woman *(2007)*

Writing in 2007, Susan Durber said 'an entirely conventional sermon may take on new resonances as it is delivered by a person whose body presents an unconventional icon of authority' (xii). It is not only how we interpret and preach from the Bible that affects what is heard. The very fact that we are women influences how our congregations hear us. In response, women preachers have stressed similarity to, rather than difference from, men preachers, and have thus regarded particularly feminine characteristics as distracting. 'Among women in the

Church, there is still much less said about the potential of preaching for transforming faith and worship than, for example, about prayers, art or poetry. There is some evidence that many women who preach do not enjoy it and that some of these women regard preaching as a task less appropriate or "natural" to themselves than to their male colleagues' (2). Granted, more than a decade has passed since these words were penned, and in some places things may have changed. It remains true, however, that the burgeoning body of work on women's preaching focuses largely on whether it is permissible and how it is heard, rather than why it is needed and how women preachers might find their own voices. For Durber a key reason for women to preach as women was so 'that the experience of men must no longer be understood as the paradigm of all human experience' (71). The Bible in a woman's sermon must be interpreted in the light of a woman's experience.

Jennifer Copeland: Feminine Registers: The Importance of Women's Voices for Christian Preaching *(2014)*

More women are training to preach and are preaching, yet what 'has yet to be critically examined ... is the constellation of meaning influenced by gender-related issues of authority and self-disclosure in the act of preaching' (xi). As more women have been accepted for training in the past few decades, the key texts used by training institutions 'have paid little attention to the theological and semantic contributions of women to the proclamation of the word' (xv). Copeland identifies a need not merely to 'include women "in the company of preachers" but to craft a new register for the preaching event' (xvii). I hope that this book will go some way towards that work.

The task of the woman preacher is to acknowledge and work with the 'social forces embedded in her life affording her a particular "standpoint". She is to 'announce to the ecclesial public her own narrative springing from the truth of her own story' (55).

Summarizing where we are

Christian feminist theology requires us to make a response to the Bible, and the way it has traditionally been used. As preachers, we need to identify our Position, as one source in my model of Theological Reflection names it. We need to be clear about our own approach to the Bible, and how we filter what we read. As we come to exegete a passage in preparation for preaching we have, I think, three alternatives: rejection, repatriation or redemption.

Some reject the Bible and faith based on it. A hermeneutic of suspicion, to coin Ricoeur's phrase, seeks to uncover hidden meanings, and avoids reading the text 'plain'. It has led some to doubt the efficacy of a male saviour for oppressed women, and to the rejection of what they perceive as an irrevocably and irredeemably sexist Bible. Mary Daly and Daphne Hampson are prominent examples of feminist theologians who chose this route.

Others seek to repatriate it, send it back to the time and land from which it came and assert that it really doesn't say much to us today. Or at least large chunks of it don't. David was a great man after God's own heart, God's chosen king. Did he hush up the rape of his daughter by his son? 'Well, that's the way it was then.' Did he cause a woman he spotted from his rooftop to be brought to his bedroom, somehow causing her to become pregnant? 'Just a sign of the times.' Did Paul say women shouldn't teach men? 'We know better these days.'

Both of these strategies risk making the Bible seem irrelevant to our congregations. How are they to know what to read seriously and what to reject, if we apparently reject bits we don't like?

Finally, others seek to redeem the Bible, wrestling with the tricky texts, the *Texts of Terror* as Phyllis Trible called them (1984), and redeem them. This is the route I have chosen. I work to find liberation for women in the text of Scripture. My motivation is to speak *for* justice. Not by constantly talking *about* justice. Not by constantly referring to oppressions and inequalities, but by trying to let different voices be heard.

It is not the purpose of this chapter, or this book, to offer a technical examination of exegetical methodology. Let me offer here a brief overview of how biblical interpretation has developed and how it might have worked to silence women.

In ancient times (roughly 150 BCE–100 CE) sacred text was read figuratively. Mystery was characteristic of Scripture. God was seen as the speaker but humans were the writers and so a multiplicity of meaning was to be expected. Earliest biblical interpretation reflected this kind of reading. Philo of Alexandria demonstrated how the Jewish Scriptures spoke to the concerns of the Graeco-Roman world, for example. It would take a different book entirely to discuss the roles of women in the Graeco-Roman world of that time, they were many and various. It is worth noting, however, the way that Aristotle presented marriage. 'A man rules ... his wife in a political way ... For the male is, by nature, more suited for rule than the female' (Aristotle, *Pol.* 1.12, 1259a39b10, cited by Riesbeck, 2015). He proposed the idea of 'marital art', which included both ruling the wife and caring for her (Cumming, 1973).

Some Jewish sects, notably the Essenes, read the Hebrew Scriptures as though the ancient texts predicted events unfolding during the lifetime of the community. A basic premise of the Dead Sea Scrolls is that the inspired text speaks to the cultural or historical situation of the interpreter in such a way that they share in the inspiration and discern what cannot otherwise have been seen in the text. There are parallels here with some contemporary preaching methods.

Early Christian interpretation (100–600 CE) treated Scripture retrospectively, as giving voice to their understanding. Thus, in the Hebrew Bible (Old Testament) the early Christians found prophecies and promises that they believed were fulfilled in Christ. Again, there are contemporary examples of this kind of interpretation. During roughly the same period Jewish exegesis turned to a method of interpreting Scripture that involved reading one text in the light of others, so the whole canon was self-interpreting.

During the first five centuries of Christianity the Church expected that, despite sometimes contentious differences in interpretation, the truth would be found in the Bible. It became the orthodox position that interpretation should be consistent with the teaching of the apostles. By the second century, Irenaeus of Lyon could write of God the Father, God the Son and God the Holy Spirit as foundations of the faith. God the Son became 'a man among men'; and through the Holy Spirit 'the patriarchs were taught about God' (Ireneaus 1952: 6–7). So the early Church read Christian theology into their Scriptures, the Hebrew Bible. Where they could find a reference to Jesus, the text was to be read literally (always bearing in mind genre and figurative expression); where they could not, the text was to be taken figuratively.

In the fifth century, Augustine proposed a way of reading the Bible that resonates with pastoral preaching. Interpretation should make a difference, it should lead to closer obedience to Jesus. Augustine was more subtle than the application model of preaching. The reader needed to have a living relationship with the text. In Augustine's model the reader of the Bible needed to be a Christian before the text itself could speak of Christ. Hear what Augustine had to say about women, before deciding whether he intended Scripture to speak to us: 'Only man is fully created in the image of God.' 'The female state is deformity.' 'The woman herself alone is not the image of God, whereas the man alone is the image of God as fully and completely as when the woman is joined with him.'

Thomas Aquinas (1225–74) suggested that biblical texts had multiple meanings, each of which could provide the basis of a distinct theology. He also said women were 'defective and misbegotten ... biologically, spiritually and intellectually inferior'. He did admit of their necessity, however: 'needed to preserve the species and provide food and drink'.

Medieval exegesis took the truth of Scripture to be what human sense could discern – the Bible meant what it said. The historical method began to gain the primacy in exegetical theory that it held for several hundred years. The year 1500 CE marked the beginning of the modern era of biblical interpretation. Historical criticism spread like wildfire, encompassing the analysis of language, history, culture. The human mind was regarded as a more reliable interpreter of Scripture than authoritarian institutions. It was based on scientific method and the presumption of objective distance between the reader and the text. It is a distance that historical criticism has not closed, and one that makes the Bible seem remote from contemporary readers. Liberation theologian Gustavo Gutiérrez commented that, 'The question we face … is not so much how to talk of God in a world come of age, but how to proclaim God as Father in an inhuman world? How do we tell the "non-persons" that they are the sons and daughters of God?' (1999: 28).

Walter Wink, progressive Christian theologian, declared historical biblical criticism bankrupt 'in the "exact" sense of the term'. A bankrupt business has only one thing wrong, he said, 'it is no longer able to accomplish its avowed purpose'. 'Biblical criticism … is bankrupt solely because it is incapable of achieving what most of its practitioners considered its purpose to be: so to interpret the Scriptures that the past becomes alive and illumines our present with new possibilities for personal and social transformation' (1973: 1).

Some Bible women

One of my ambitions might be to imitate Jenni Murray's two books *The History of Britain in 21 Women* and *The History of the World in 21 Women* by producing a 'History of the Bible in 21 Women'. The woman who touched the hem of Jesus' garment would certainly be among them. She had bled for 12 years, handed over all her money to physicians who could do nothing, and would have been ostracized from the synagogue and the community, having to walk down the street shouting 'unclean' at anyone whose path she crossed. She got fed up with it, pushed through the crowd and touched the hem of Jesus' garment. And Jesus stopped Jairus, the synagogue leader, in his tracks, and listened to this woman's story. Perhaps that is part of our calling as Jesus modelled it – to stop, and listen to women's stories.

Another woman who would make it into my book of 21 would be Ruth. I think women preachers can learn quite a lot from Ruth's story. I have certainly come to love it. Read without taking any notice of the titles various translators have stuck in, some of Ruth's attributes stand out more clearly.

First, she persists. The first parallel I want to draw between Ruth and women preachers is this – Ruth gleans among the sheaves and behind the reapers. In other words, she looks for grain after the best has apparently been gathered up and after other workers have gone ahead of her. It doesn't look very promising. It sometimes feels like that when I come to the Bible trying to be faithful to the call to be a woman preacher. It's hard to find new things to say, ways of interpreting the text that don't simply pass on somebody else's words, or some androcentric doctrine. I sometimes feel trapped by traditional readings of stories with which I feel profoundly uncomfortable, but can't immediately see a different way of reading. Ruth doesn't only glean among and behind, she also gleans till late. She works persistently to find what she needs, something that will set Naomi free.

Because Ruth persists she is able also to see into the needs of others. Naomi says, in various places, that she is empty, afflicted, bitter and abandoned by God. Naomi, in many ways, characterizes the woman (most of us) whose identity is constructed, by others at least, around our gender identity and the stereotypes that go with it. Women leaders are expected to be pastoral, for example. It's interesting that although Ruth sticks with Naomi and ensures she is fed, she does not put her own life on hold in order to satisfy Naomi's needs. Just as Ruth had to take responsibility for making her own choice, so Naomi has to choose at the end of the story whether to remain bitter and abandoned or whether to accept her new freedom. Ruth promotes the well-being of Naomi not only by caring for her but by giving her a voice.

Then, Ruth speaks the truth. We take her response to Boaz for granted, somewhat. At first she seems to respond with something akin to servility when Boaz speaks to her: 'Why have I found favour in your sight, that you should take notice of me, when I am a foreigner?' (3.10). But when Boaz explains that he has heard of her and her loyalty to Naomi she goes on to say something like, 'Well that's great. Long may it continue. You have put me at my ease by speaking kindly to me.' Despite Boaz's apparently high position socially, Ruth tells him how it is.

At the start of the story she is clear with Naomi. She goes on to speak truth to Boaz not only in her words but in her actions too. She makes clear what she wants, both in the fields and on the threshing floor. Integrity is essential to her success – and ours. It is even important that the image we portray is consistent with our speech and our actions. And we have to be able to verbalize our theology and our reading of the Bible clearly and consistently if we are going to undermine the effects of sexism on ourselves and on others.

There is a strong correlation between who we are, how we look and what we say. The moment we allow comments about our appearance, the way we speak or what we say to silence us, the 'divine floods of light and life no longer flow into our souls', to quote an early suffragette, Elizabeth Cady Stanton.

Ruth persists, she promotes the cause of others, she speaks truth and she subverts culture. Her culture, and ours, her 'church' and ours, perpetuate the myth that self-sacrifice is inherent in women. The story of Ruth is sometimes even preached that way. She left her home and remains loyal to Naomi, after all. But she also seduces a wealthy single man over whom her position (as Naomi's daughter-in-law) gives her some influence. This is a culture where women were more or less possessions to be traded among men as they saw fit. A culture where men could seduce women without obligation. Yet she overturns it. She seduces the man, and then she asks for something in return.

I don't want to push this too far, but it is a fact that in Hebrew feet are used euphemistically for another body part, so when the book of Ruth tells us its hero covered Boaz's feet it quite probably means something different. I lived in France for a short time and once had the opportunity to go to a grape harvest celebration. I saw a lot of things going on, but not much foot covering.

So what is required of us as women preachers living under a patriarchal narrative?

We have to persist.
We have to promote the cause of the voiceless.
We are to speak truth.
We are to subvert culture.

It is best summed up in the final paragraph of Jennifer Copeland's *Feminine Registers* (2014):

Power is less about control and dominion and more about the capacity to produce change. Those on the margins – in this case, women – bring the transformational potential with them and offer it to those in the center ... The result is not that women are better preachers than men but that preachers, men and women, will become better when different voices interface with one another, transforming our understanding of one another and of God.

Time for reflection

This reflection is based on Silencing Women, and offers an opportunity to face our own silencing.

How am I silenced?

1. A poem about sexism in the Church:

> A meeting. The leadership.
> Shepherds of the flock.
> Carers.
> Discerning God's will.
> Defining the path.
> Praying.
> As we depart
> A hand squeezes my breast
> A voice says 'It's OK, isn't it?'
> 'You don't mind.'
> And the men don't notice
> And the women are not there.
>
> A gathering. Ministers.
> Feeders of the flock.
> Celebrants.
> Ready with bread and with wine.
> Preparing to remember
> The night when he was betrayed.
> One, robed, squeezes my hand
> And his voice says 'I can't take bread and wine from you.'
> 'It's OK, isn't it?'
> 'You don't mind.'
> And the men don't notice
> And the women are not there.
>
> A gathering. A crowd.
> Welcoming.

Excluding.
He a synagogue leader.
She a decade unclean.
A hand stretched.
Healing received.
The Teacher stoops, listens.
This woman is noticed.
And, for a moment, this man is not there.

The poem speaks of everyday sexism in the Church, contrasting it with the way Jesus spoke with a woman. The first two verses resonate for many of us, while we yearn for something like the encounter in the final verse. *When have you been silenced by a patriarchal narrative? How does your experience enable you to speak out, or offer hope to others?*

2. Think about your preaching, review the last few sermons you have preached. *Where have you been silent about gender injustice? Where have you intentionally looked for, and included, a woman's perspective?*

Notes

1 Letter responding to Caroline Kennard explaining his views on women, held in University of Cambridge archives.

2 CODEC Research Centre for Digital Theology and The College of Preachers.

4

Hearing Women's Faith

Narratives

In the last chapter we saw how a patriarchal narrative under-pins much of our thinking in media, science, the arts and religion. We also looked at how patriarchy is supported by sexism.

In this chapter I want to look at how the same narrative influences our interpretation and transmission of the Christian faith. In particular, I want to think about women's experiences of God, life and sin, and what that might mean for women's preaching. In order that my argument is not dismissed simply as a matter of opinion, I will base a good deal of what I want to say on research evidence.

I need to clarify what I mean by 'narrative', before we go further. The period between the Middle Ages and the early twentieth century is often referred to as 'Modernity'. It was a time when, across Europe, the narrative of a God-ordained social structure dominated by Church and Crown was challenged. The age of 'this must be so, because the Church said it' was over, and people were encouraged to think for themselves. The ethos of the new era, Modernity, is encapsulated in Descartes' well-known proposition 'I think, therefore I am', and is characterized by a painting, housed in London's National Gallery, *Experiment with an Air Pump*. In it an ordinary family, from Derbyshire, sit around a kitchen table depriving a bird of oxygen, in order to observe what happens. The act of experimentation is portrayed as an almost religious event, surrounded by light – an illustration of human rationalism replacing institutional authority as the means of finding truth.

Many of the ways in which preaching and teaching in the Church developed were influenced by the new narrative. In a rational age it was thought necessary to be able to give an intelligent defence of the faith. Part of this development required objective argument, and objectivity is always defined by the dominant thought forms of the time, as we saw with the development of Darwin's theory of evolution. Thus, 'women are frequently required not only to justify their stories in a male-dominated institution, but also to express them in the language and thought-forms of male-dominated philosophical, psychological and religious traditions' (Bennett, 2002: 40).

The reasoned approach was not without merit. It presented the Christian faith appropriately to contemporary culture. An unintentional consequence, however, was that the faith was reduced to a series of doctrinal propositions.

The catastrophes of the First and Second World Wars challenged Modernity's narrative. Human beings did not behave entirely rationally, and were capable of great cruelty even in so-called advanced times. The problem with Modernity, according to Lyotard, who first formulated a definition of Postmodernism, was that its legitimacy lay 'not in an original founding act, but in a future to be accomplished ... in an Idea to be realised', so any assurance of its rightness lies in the future (1979: 18).

We live now in a time when the Modernist narrative seems increasingly questionable; a time of 'Postmodernism' (this is a slippery, contended term, but here is not the place to explore it). Because I sometimes think in pictures, Postmodernism, it seems to me, looks Modernism in the eye, raises a brow and asks quizzically: 'Really?' Where Modernism makes universalizing claims (knowledge will be discovered rationally and will lead to human progress), Postmodernism is acutely aware of situatedness – where we are in culture, in tradition, in experience and in position. For me, Postmodernism's raised eyebrow is quizzical rather than cynical. It does not dismiss truth but rather takes it so seriously that we are liberated to go back to basics and rediscover what it might mean. The four-source model of theological reflection that I prefer enables us to engage in this kind of thinking, using a cultural perspective to raise an eyebrow at tradition, or personal experience to quiz culture, for example.

Progress remains part of an overarching narrative, despite our questions. It underpins many theories of human development, and that is where we go next.

Stages, seasons and maturity

Ideas about how human beings mature bear a resemblance to evolutionary theory – we start out naive, immature, incapable, and become wise, mature and able. Maturation follows some kind of orderly consistent sequence through identifiable stages, regardless of context. Piaget (1929, 1962) initiated the development of 'stage' concepts with his cognitive development theory. He envisaged cognitive development as a progressive reorganization of thinking caused by biological maturing and cultural engagement. Kohlberg (1981, 1984) extended the theory to incorporate moral development. He suggested that as children mature, their moral reasoning becomes more sophisticated. He tested this out using what is known as 'Heinz's dilemma'. Kohlberg presented children with this story: Heinz's wife was dying from a particular form of cancer. A drug that was her only hope had been developed by a local chemist. Heinz tried to buy some, but the chemist was selling it for ten times the cost of production, and Heinz could not afford it. He raised half the money, with help from family and friends. He explained to the chemist that his wife was dying and asked whether he could have the drug cheaper or pay the rest of the money later. The chemist refused, saying that as he had discovered the drug he deserved to make money from it. The desperate husband broke into the chemist's and stole the drug. Working with a sample of 72 boys, Kohlberg identified three levels of moral reasoning, each with two sub-stages. At the Pre-Conventional stage, children have no personal morality, and are instead shaped by rules and the consequences of breaking them. The next stage, Conventional Morality, where Kohlberg located most adolescents and adults, moral standards are internalized but not questioned, and reasoning is based on the norms of the group. Level 3, Post-conventional Morality, is only achievable by 10–15 per cent of people, according to the theory. It is where reasoning and judgement are based on self-chosen principles.

This kind of generalized staged development can be seen in spiritual theories such as Fowler's *Stages of Faith* (1981), which suggests that 'faith stages ... provide generalisable, formal descriptions of integrated sets of operations of knowing and valuing ... related in a sequence we believe to be invariant' (99–100). In other words, everyone develops in the same way. Adapting Kohlberg's theory, Fowler also suggests that not everyone will achieve the highest level of maturity. Scott Peck subsequently popularized these stages in his book *The Different Drum*.

A significant problem with Kohlberg's theory, and those based on it, arises for women. Maturity is reached via stages in which the individual 'moves on' from prioritizing happy, healthy interpersonal relationships to focusing on societal order and the maintenance of individual rights. At about the time when people might be expected to move through these stages, women are being drafted into new primary and secondary caring roles as grandparents and carers for elderly parents. In the UK one in four women aged 50–64 has caring responsibilities for older relatives,[1] while around two-thirds of grandparents (mostly grandmothers) help with childcare.[2] Thus the effect of maturation ideas based on Kohlberg's stages is that women seem to display impaired maturity. Carol Gilligan in particular has critiqued such theories as biased towards white men. She proposed just three stages of moral development – selfishness, social morality and principled morality. In *In a Different Voice* (1982), Gilligan pointed out that Kohlberg had developed his theory working only with boys. His scoring method favoured what he regarded as objective reasoning over decision-making based on relationship, which would, according to Gilligan, suit girls better.

In contrast to cognitive stage theory are psychodynamic theories. They form a loose network of related ideas that emphasize the role of relationship and self-identity in human development. The underlying assumption is that behaviour and emotions are rooted in childhood experiences. All behaviour has a cause. Personality has three parts: Id, the biological components and personality traits present at birth; Ego, which develops to mediate between Id and the external world; and Superego, which incorporates the values and morals learned from others. Jungian psychology, focusing on personality development (Id), is of particular interest in Christian spirituality and pastoral care since it is the foundation of the popular Myers–Briggs Personality Type Indicator. Jung proposed that apparently random behaviours are actually prompted by the ways in which people use their mental capacities. He defined two basic functions – taking in information (perceiving) and organizing it (judging). Individuals perform these functions according to their 'preferences'. While everyone both perceives and judges, some prefer one function while others prefer the other. Jung also observed that, 'Each person seems to be energised more by either the external world (extraversion) or the internal world (introversion).' His theory of psychological typology was published in 1921. Subsequently Isabel Briggs Myers and Katharine Cook Briggs developed the theory to produce a typology indicator aimed at enabling people to understand themselves better. The enneagram, which performs a similar function and is preferred by spiritual leaders such as Richard Rohr, is also based on a structural model that seeks to encompass the whole human experience.

As with cognitive stage theory, psychodynamic theories raise important issues for women. Jean Baker Miller (1976) demonstrated how women had been marginalized in their development by judging their experiences from a male perspective. Chodorow (1978) differentiated between the experiences

of boys and girls, proposing that girls recognize their membership of the female world, and therefore mature in connectedness
to their mother, where boys recognize their difference and
measure maturity in terms of separation.

Nicola Slee (2004) questioned existing theories from a feminist perspective, suggesting that generalized theories do not allow
for 'relational knowing' (a term proposed by Fowler himself in
2000 as a way of making his model more inclusive). Invariant
stages, she concluded, do not account for 'women's distinctive
patterns of faith', particularly in the middle stages of movement towards separation and autonomy. Other women writers
maintain the idea of spiritual development stages, but suggest
that they are more flexible in women. Whatever conclusion we
reach as women, in the light of Postmodern scepticism towards
overarching truth, faith stage theories seem reproachable for
their universalizing nature. Nowadays, we are more likely to
want to say that not everyone is the same, rather than to seek
normative structures.

What does this have to do with preaching?

First, as preachers, we need a clear model of maturity and
discipleship. I recall hearing one clergyperson deride the congregation as 'commitment averse'. They had been trying to
encourage their hearers to do more, to engage with the local
community. Other versions of a similar clergy-led refrain might
bemoan low attendance at home groups or lack of involvement
in church activities. There are other church growth strategies
that encourage leaders to get the men first, and the women will
follow, and the dominant model in the Church of England cur-
rently seems to be get the young and forget the old. I wonder
how an honest appraisal of the lives of 'sandwich carers' might
affect what we say from the front. How might we preach to a
group of people responsible for grandchild care, parent care
and a part-time job all at the same time? Would we demand
more? Or might we seek to reassure and encourage? Perhaps
even commend a Sabbath rest to them, while upholding their
service to others as a model worth following?

Second, the realization that universalizing models of faith

development are based on the experience of certain men should lead us to edit out of all our sermons phrases that suggest generalized understandings – phrases such as 'we all', or even just 'we' when it implies everyone is the same! Just as the modernist preacher suggests 'I'm sure we all ...', the Postmodern hearer thinks, 'No, we don't.'

Maturity does not look the same for everyone, and widely accepted models do not seem to account for women's experiences of faith.

If we turn to the New Testament, however, a different type of maturity seems to be depicted. Paul berates the Corinthian church for their failure to mature. They still need to be fed on milk, rather than solid food (1 Cor. 3.2). In his later letter to the same church, he prays that they might become perfect by recognizing their own weaknesses (2 Cor. 13.9). The letter to the church in Ephesus seems to characterize wisdom as knowledge of God's power and commitment to church unity. A whistle-stop tour through the epistle suggests the centrality of relationship: heaven and earth will be in unity (1.10); we, as unique individuals, are united in the body of Christ (2.10); unity establishes the commonwealth of God on earth (3.10). In order to establish this revolutionary unity, we are to challenge lies and seek out truth (4.15); to live in the power of the resurrection (5.14); and in order to do it we should put on the armour of God (6.13). Although New Testament writers offer no specific structure or manifestation of individual maturity, it seems to me that relationship plays a central part, something that, as we will see, is central to women's faith development.

Before we move on, I want to illustrate this point with a sermon snippet. I had been invited to preach on Ephesians 4.17–31, and given the title 'Do not grieve the Holy Spirit'. My colleague, preaching at a different service, focused on what maturity looks like in terms of behaviour. Their underlying assumption was that it looked the same for everyone. In my sermon I focused on the relational aspect of unity and faith. This is not an overtly feminist sermon but it does, I think, illustrate how a woman's perspective affects what we say:

Sermon snippet

Let's start at the beginning – Ephesians 1.10. God's plan in Christ was to gather all things in heaven and earth in him. God's eternal plan is to bring together everything in heaven and on earth into unity. The whole of creation is united in Christ on earth. Unfortunately, what human beings have done is kick God upstairs out of sight so that we don't have to take too seriously the concept of oneness. But oneness, unity, in this case between heaven and earth, is an essential part of the theology of Ephesians.

The theme continues in Ephesians 2.10: 'For we are what he has made us, created in Christ Jesus for good works, which God prepared beforehand to be our way of life.' Just as humankind has reduced the eternal plan of God to a migration from earth to heaven, and kept God out of the way in the world, so the idea of being created in Christ for good works has been reduced to a kind of morality – 'do this' but 'don't do that'. But that isn't anything like what the writer says here. What they say is, 'You are God's poem, God's innovation.' Each of us is made uniquely, a poem of God, to do what only we can do on this earth. We are each called to be who only we can be – to play our own full part in the body of Christ. Unity, oneness, is now applied to the relationship between God and God's creatures. We are empowered by the Spirit of God to live out who we were meant to be.

The writer makes this radical unity – unity of the whole of creation, unity between God and God's creatures, and unity among human beings – the basis of their theology. Speaking the truth in love means working out how this affects what we do and say.

We have been marked with the Holy Spirit of God, as signs and symbols of this unity that is the mark and substance of the reign of God. If that is true then the way we live and speak and relate should be a sign of the redemption of the unity of all things – heaven and earth, the person we are and the person we have been made to be, the commonwealth of God and the world in which we live.

Anything that causes disunity grieves the Spirit. That means that God is involved in every aspect of life, every aspect. Christian behaviour is not about keeping some kind of moral code – not doing this or that. It is about living in harmony with God through the power of the Spirit.

Whenever we do something that divides us from another, we grieve the Spirit. Whenever we live as though God is not involved in the world, we grieve the Spirit. Whenever we think of ourselves as less than God's unique creation, we grieve the Spirit.

It's the little things that divide – the neighbour who parks a bit inconveniently becomes the idiot who shouldn't be allowed a car; the politician who stands for something we disagree with becomes the potential tyrant who should be run out of office; the earth is important and should be cared for, but I do need an extra carrier bag from the supermarket; those Christians over there don't do things the way I like them, so they are wrong – in fact, they are probably dangerous and I should speak against them.

Me? I'm just a housewife, or mother. When we phone somebody, 'Hello, it's just me'. That grieves the Holy Spirit too.

What difference does it make?

If women's development and experiences are distinctive, how does that difference translate into experiences of faith and God. In my sermon snippet above, I attempted to respond to the findings of earlier writers in my final sentence:

The time I have spent listening to women's stories has convinced me that there are distinctly feminine patterns of sinfulness, and that pride is not women's besetting sin ... even as they talk of pride they are feeling worthless and powerless. (Guenther, 1992: 134)

When we talk about women's faith experiences, what do we mean? What is it that is distinctive? My sermon snippet above illustrates a little of what I mean, in the final sentences: 'Me? I'm just a housewife, or mother. When we phone somebody, "Hello, it's just me". That grieves the Holy Spirit too.' Writing in 1960, Valerie Saiving suggested 'the temptations of woman *as woman* are not the same as the temptations of man *as man*'. Sin, she says, is widely defined as 'the self's attempt ... to magnify its own power, righteousness or knowledge'. It is identified with self-assertion while love is characterized as selflessness (37). Such definitions are not helpful for women, she believes. Our tendency is not towards thinking too much of ourselves, pride, but of thinking too little.

While many Christians are familiar with Romans 12.3, 'I say to everyone among you not to think of yourself more highly than you ought to think', and often interpret it as an injunction to humility, I suspect that in a slightly wider context, its meaning changes:

> Do not be conformed to this world, but be transformed by the renewing of your minds, so that you may discern what is the will of God – what is good and acceptable and perfect.
>
> For by the grace given to me I say to everyone among you not to think of yourself more highly than you ought to think, but to think with sober judgement, each according to the measure of faith that God has assigned. For as in one body we have many members, and not all the members have the same function. (vv. 2–4)

For many women it is the earlier exhortation to be transformed, to have our minds renewed and to discern what is good and acceptable to God that matters. For so many of our hearers, it is the assurance that sober judgement will result in them learning to value themselves. It is the woman who thinks too little of herself who is 'good and acceptable'. If, as I have sought to show, widely accepted models of moral and spiritual development fail to place equal value on women's experiences, Christian women inhabit a world where our understanding of God, faith and sin is not spoken of. Preaching for women must be truthful, recognizing 'the importance of attending to real women in the real world, to a realistic assessment of sin and salvation, of evil and goodness as they are made manifest in women's actual lives' (Bennett, 2002: 97).

Considering worthlessness and powerlessness as sin proves challenging for some. Indeed, the valuing of such characteristics seems firmly rooted in the overriding narrative of the Church. Interviewing a woman in her eighties, Abby Day traced ideas of protection and permission. Since marriage this woman had never had paid work: 'my husband wouldn't allow it'. She counted herself blessed because she had been 'very well looked after' by her father and then her husband. After having a stroke her husband became very protective and did not allow her to do things for herself. If she tried to stand he would say 'sit!' as though speaking to a dog. When asked about God this same woman said, 'I think it's a he' and spoke of God's protection in terms similar to those used of her father and husband. Women, in this narrative, need to be protected – we are powerless.

Some would claim that the Church is becoming feminized. Podles (1999), for example, claimed correlation between the ordination of women in the Church of England and the decline in male attendance, claiming that ordination of female priests in 1994 led to an increase in female-to-male church attendance from 55–45 to 63–37.8. 'The Church of England is quickly becoming a church of women, by women, for women,' he said (20). The problem is that although women might attend church in greater numbers, the Church remains dominated by men. Actual figures show that over recent years the proportion of women ordinands has remained around 40 per cent, leaving us in a significant minority. Women ordained to stipendiary roles are significantly less than men. About equal numbers of women are ordained to stipendiary and self-supporting posts, while two-thirds of men are stipendiary. Since the consecration of the first woman bishop in 2015, 18 more women have become bishops, while 23 new male bishops have been chosen. Of these, five women and seven men became diocesan bishops. Although women remain a minority, the picture does seem to be changing.

As a result of ordination figures, many women Christians do not identify themselves with those who run their church and teach their faith. Indeed, they often feel that their own expressions of faith are judged inadequate. Examples of this can be found in the way small groups are regarded. More women than men are part of homegroups of one kind or another. When asked, many account for their membership of a group in terms of support, although significant numbers might also speak of encouragement in discipleship or learning. In his study of small groups in America, sociologist Robert Wuthnow concluded that groups dominated by women were lacking in theological rigour, because 'the sacred comes to be associated with small insights that seem intuitively correct to the small group rather than wisdom accrued over the centuries in hermitages, seminaries, universities, congregations and church councils' (1994: 358). It is interesting to note that at least four of these five sources of wisdom have been male dominated for most of their history. In this study, experiences specific to women are deemed unsuitable for inclusion in small group discussion. The names given to small groups are also indicative of the value placed on them. While evening groups might be labelled study, home or cell groups, those taking place during the day frequently bear names such as 'Mum and Tot', or 'Baby and Bible', thus identifying the group by a particular attribute of its members, rather than by its function or location. In many local churches the model of small groups is one of central control. The content and pattern of the evening is issued from the leadership, with freedom to talk about group concerns being limited. Hence when Anna Strhan researched a city-centre evangelical church she found that what the leadership reported 'the church' believed did not match up with what the people themselves said. Women's experiences are often, intentionally or otherwise, written out of small group faithing because the 'standards' are male normative. The predominant culture has 'rendered [women's] lives "unspeakable"' (Graham, 2014: 198).

How might we speak of women's lives? I was once asked to preach in a church where the leader was about to retire. They had given many years of dedicated, unpaid service and were keen that the church should continue. Unfortunately, the congregation consisted largely of elderly people with waning energy and frequent illness. The passage I was given was Matthew 14.22–33, variously entitled 'Jesus walks on Water', or 'Peter walks on Water'. Like you, I have heard many an injunction to 'get out of the boat' if you want to walk on water. The focus of almost every sermon I have ever heard on this passage has been Peter's heroics. Yet, being conscious of my congregation and of my women's spirituality that said women, in particular, are pretty good at feeling inadequate, I wondered if there was something new I could find in this simple story.

Sermon snippet

Peter seems to grasp at the possibility that it is the Lord, and tests it out. 'If it is you, call me to you.' And Jesus does.

Suddenly Peter realizes what he is doing and begins to sink so that he has to call out to Jesus to save him.

And apparently, although Peter has believed that it really was Jesus, and has got out of the boat, and has walked on the water, and has put his trust in Jesus far more than the others who stayed in the boat … Jesus ticks him off. 'You of little faith, why did you doubt?'

Is that really how it happened? Or can we read the story differently?

Could it be that instead of it being Peter who had the faith, it was the others? Wasn't Peter being a bit like the annoying show-off waving his hand in the air and shouting 'pick me, pick me'? Was it at this point, when Peter wanted to share in the moment with Jesus, that he most went astray? Did he want to leave the place of fear, the boat, and go to a place where he would be admired and comforted?

Surely Jesus might have considered responding with, 'Who do you think you are, Peter? Sit back down and leave this to me.' But he knew that what Peter really needed was a couple of steps on the water to help him realize who Jesus was, and a nosedive into the sea to help him realize who *he* was.

I think that is a fair reflection of what happens to us in times of fear. Jesus assures us that he is there with us, but we want to be

---

called out of that place into an easier place, a place where there are no anxieties, but where all is calm. Where we know we are close to him.

And that is our real time of doubt. It is when we are unable to trust that he is with us in the tough times and so pray to be taken out of them that we most demonstrate our lack of faith.

Perhaps it was the other disciples who showed faith. Faith enough to stay in the boat.

Perhaps rather than being a story about a heroic disciple who was willing to risk his life to demonstrate who Jesus is, this is actually a story about the other eleven, who never thought of themselves as heroes, who never dreamed of putting Jesus to the test, who were willing to keep rowing against the wind until he got into the boat with them no matter how long it took.

They were just looking for their Lord to join them where they were – and that was where the miracle happened. Not out on the water with Peter doing fancy tricks, but in the boat.

It was when Jesus joined them in the boat that the storm ceased.

Where Peter asked Jesus to do something for him, those in the boat worshipped him, 'You really are the Son of God.'

Women's faith experiences

How do women experience church-based Christian faith differently from men? In three significant ways, I think: expectations of us are distinctly different; relationship is central to our faith; and historic doctrines distance us from the Bible, and from Jesus.

A key expectation of all women, and one that many are content to voice, is that of reading ourselves in. In most congregations, women are expected to read themselves into patriarchal language. Whether the person at the front says 'Dearly beloved brethren', sings 'now I am your son, I am adopted in your family', or uniquely prays to the 'Father', women are expected to assume we are included. If we accept that pride is not a woman's sin, we are expected to read ourselves out of prayers and sermons that assume it is a deadly sin of everyone. Sometimes we are even expected to accept expert male opinion about our own lives.

We are expected to defer our needs to those of men – I recently spoke with someone who had been abused by her partner, but was told that she needed to be faithful because she was God's way of bringing him to 'Himself'. Research shows that this is not at all unusual. If our congregation reflects society as a whole, we need to be aware that 8 per cent of women (and 4 per cent of men) will be in abusive relationships.[3] A similar thing happens in preaching, where the male role predominates. I wonder how many women have been harmed by preaching that dismisses their pain. I know of several who were damaged by a preacher's interpretation of 2 Samuel 12.15–25, the death of David and Bathsheba's child. Here's an example: 'David's adulterous relationship with Bathsheba is one of the most infamous, heartbreaking events recorded in the Old Testament. The emotional pain and anguish caused by David's sin plagued the king for the remainder of his days.' The fact that David abused Bathsheba 'plagued' him! It is as though Bathsheba's pain did not exist.

In her powerful book *Scars Across Humanity*, my good friend Elaine Storkey points out, 'From early in church history, men have defined women's sexuality, and presented it as a problem' (2015: 204). The story of the Church is so shot through with women as an 'issue' that we cannot simply dismiss it by saying things are better now. Here are some examples:

Every woman should be filled with shame at the thought that she is a woman.
(Clement of Alexandria, 150–215)

You are the devil's gateway ... the image of God, the man Adam, you broke ... you deserved death ...
(Tertullian, 160–223)

What is a woman but an enemy of friendship, an inescapable punishment, a necessary evil, a natural temptation, a domestic danger, delectable mischief, a fault in nature, painted with beautiful colours? ... the whole of her body is nothing less than phlegm, blood, bile, rheum and the fluid of digested food ... (John Chrysostom, 347–407)

... while scripture on the first, third fourth and sixth days relates that having finished the works of each God saw that it was good, on the second day He omitted this altogether, leaving us to understand that two is not a good number because it prefigures the marriage contract. (Jerome, 342–420)

Woman is a misbegotten man. (Albertus Magus, 1200–80)

Feminism is a socialist, anti-family, political movement that encourages women to leave their husbands, kill their children, practice witchcraft, destroy capitalism and become lesbians. (Pat Robertson, b. 1930, American Evangelical and adviser to President Trump)

Reflecting upon the biblical data, we can see that the primary leaders and teachers of the church are to be suitably qualified men, which does not include those presenting as male by virtue of gender reassignment. (Fellowship of Independent Evangelical Churches statement 2016)

Jesus did not shrink from challenging social convention. His disciples included women as well as men. Yet he chose only men as his Apostles. (Forward in Faith 2018)

Just like Bathsheba, the biggest expectation of women in our churches seems to be that we should not mind if our experiences are ignored, we are constantly represented by the 'bad' women of the Bible, and treated as though our pain does not exist. But centuries of this kind of theological thinking, mirrored by the attitudes in the quotations above, has an effect on the churches we are part of and speak to.

Expectations of women preachers seem varied. Some time ago, Heather Walton and Susan Durber suggested in their book of women's sermons that many women had abandoned preaching altogether. In *Preaching Like a Woman*, Durber wrote, 'among women in the Church, there is still much less said about the potential of preaching for transforming faith and worship than, for example, about prayers, art or poetry. There is some evidence that many women who preach do not enjoy it and that some of these women regard preaching as a task less appropriate or "natural" to themselves than to their male colleagues' (2007: 2). We are also expected to hear critique that I suspect would not be levelled at men. On the way out of church one Sunday morning, for example, a man I had never before met said, 'That was an excellent sermon. But I have to ask, how much of it was you and how much had you lifted from elsewhere?'

The very experience of preaching as a woman seems distinctive. Virginia Purvis-Smith wrote in 2005, 'When a clergywoman preaches from a pulpit, she enters a space which has particular aesthetic value, for this space has been occupied, and its character defined by male presence for centuries' (2005: 224). We are expected not to mind when someone tells us they won't be staying for the service now they know we are preaching. 'That's all right, isn't it?' someone said to me. In their view they occupied the moral and theological high ground. And, of course, 'it isn't personal'.

One aspect of women's faith that seems frequently ignored is relationship. It is central to women's faith, according to research. Women come to faith through relationship and interpret sin as broken relationship. 'Faith is not just cognitive knowing but is … having a relationship with God, and encompassing one's commitments and values' (Joung, 2013: 162). Focusing on how women come to faith in the first place, Nicola Slee found the 'strong emphasis on the cognitive component of faith' inadequate. Among women, 'personalized and relational forms of appropriating faith' dominated (2004: 166). In contrast to Fowler's 'articulate, conceptually clear and consciously owned faith', women experience what Slee terms an 'apophatic' faith, 'aware of what it does *not* know'. Rather than being transcended as faith matures, 'women's identity, development and spirituality are embedded in a strong sense of connectedess to the other' (159). If such characteristics are key to women's faith development, and women preachers do not learn to speak of faith in these ways, women's experiences of faith are silenced.

Connectedness, relationship, seems key to biblical faith too. The Church is portrayed as 'the body of Christ' rather than a group of like-minded people (1 Cor. 12.27; Eph. 4.4). Jesus is placed by the Gospel writers in networks of relationship, and when the time came to leave his disciples, he did not instruct them with key points to remember, but gave them bread and wine to take into their bodies, or washed their feet. Preaching as a woman does not simply mean speaking *about* women's experiences of faith, but speaking *from* them too, including speaking about connectedness. Below is an extract from a sermon on 1 Corinthians 12. In it I highlight the importance of relationship rather than doctrine:

Sermon snippet

The Bible changed fundamentally in the twelfth century. And then it changed once again fundamentally in the sixteenth century. The two changes made it a very different kind of text.

They were in many ways profoundly unhelpful.

But we read the Bible now as though they really matter!

I'm talking about the arbitrary division of the text into chapters and verses. Chapters were introduced in the twelfth century and verses in the sixteenth. And the effect has been to mislead us. We start reading at the beginning of a chapter, irrespective of the fact that it doesn't make sense.

That's what happens with our reading this morning. It appears at first sight as though Paul is setting out on a treatise to explain the gifts of the Spirit to the church in Corinth.

He isn't. What we have read is simply an outworking of the more important point Paul has already written about – it is the application of Paul's theology. And in Corinthians Paul's theology is that we are the body of Christ. We collectively are one body. We collectively are the temple of the Holy Spirit. God works in each of us. Each of us has the same authority, the same blessing, the same position in the Church. Leaders are no more important than anyone else, and to treat other believers, other members of the body, as expendable is to live by a false gospel. We all belong together.

One body.

That is Paul's theology.

And then he goes on to explain how we might then live. Before this bit about spiritual gifts he has already talked about living out a servant faith in our bodies. Not pushing forward at communion. Not shouting louder than other people who might be praying at the same time as us. In other words, being mutually submissive. After all, all the children of Israel were under the cloud, for protection. And all the children of Israel went through the waters of the sea together. You have heard the expression there is no 'I' in team. Well for Paul, there is no 'I' in church either. We are all one in Christ Jesus.

Having dealt with all of these other issues Paul comes to spiritual gifts. The passage read this morning.

And this is what he says – obviously there are different kinds of gift. But why are they given?

For the common good.

That's it.

Varieties of service, varieties of gift, varieties of activity. It seems to resonate with the twenty-first-century mantra 'we're all different'. 'So you are,' Paul would say, 'but you belong together.'

Women, then, have expectations placed on us by the Church, and experience faith as relationship. Finally, the espoused doctrine of the Church can distance us from the Bible and from Jesus. When women's faith is not expressed in preaching or found in exegesis, it can seem distant from the faith of the Church. Where are women disciples to find role models either in church or in the Bible? We seem to be trapped in a male-dominated cycle – God became human in the form of a man, Jesus; God is therefore male; male is therefore a characteristic of God. While it would be naive to say that all women role models are good for all women, it is nevertheless the case that women in the Bible are either ignored or rendered weak.

Let's take as an example, Joanna, a woman mentioned by Luke (8.1–3). At first sight Luke describes a group who had previously been healed by Jesus and subsequently cared for him and his followers from their possessions. Already the women and men disciples are differentiated: the men had been called to discipleship, they follow out of faith; the women had benefited from healing, they follow out of gratitude. Why does healing and gratitude devalue what the women do? At the time women were the possession either of their father or their husband. If they were damaged in some way, compensation was payable. But if the damage was caused by illness or demon possession, there was no one from whom compensation could be claimed, and the women may become unwanted. The discipleship of these women might be devalued because they were without home or family, having nowhere to go, and therefore needing to follow Jesus.

Another way in which Joanna and the others are silenced in this passage is the role they are deemed, by some, to play. Providing for Jesus and his disciples out of their resources might suggest that they rendered material care, and were not involved in Jesus' ministry. A common reading of these verses seems to go something like this: 'Jesus and the twelve went out on mission, and incidentally, because they were so grateful to him/them, the women tagged along and did chores for them.'

The sentence which occupies the first three verses of chapter 8 can be interpreted in two ways. All the women might have provided for all the men, or the unnamed women provided for Jesus, the twelve and the named women. Evidence from elsewhere in Luke suggests that he does not expect all women to behave in the same way; the story of Mary and Martha for example, shows two different behaviours. From this perspective the named women, Mary Magdalene, Joanna and

Susanna, might have roles other than waiting on the men. The word Luke uses in verse 3 is *diakonos*, which primarily means not servant but herald or messenger. In this case the women, at least the named women, were involved in preaching, being messengers of the good news. In fact, successors to Elizabeth and Mary in the ministry of the commonwealth of God. So, while there are examples of women taking part in the ministry of Jesus during his lifetime, the interpretation of biblical texts has distanced them from our contemporary readings.

Communality

It cannot be enough, then, that women preach in the same way as men, with some kind of holy caveat that 'of course women's experience is of value too'. If women's experience is genuinely valued it must be spoken of clearly. The question is, how?

Early feminism determined to make explicit and visible the stories of women's lives in order to validate their experiences. Later feminists became aware of the risks involved in assuming essential or fixed female identities or experiences, and turned towards more individualistic ideals. The call for women to preach differently or to speak of women's experiences risks essentialism, in the same way as early feminism risked privileging women over men. While such a strategy might benefit women, it might equally exclude men from the Christian community. While both the woman preacher and women hearers are part of the sermon, no experience of life or faith should be imposed on the whole congregation.

If we are to preach in ways that treat women's experiences seriously, and that include all our hearers, we have to avoid generalizing narratives and particularizing essentialism. Traditional models of preaching address issues of commonality by considering what the congregation has in common either as an assembly of the faithful, or in common with people in Scripture. This model can lead to simplistic equivalences between what happens in a Bible story or to a Bible character and what that might mean for the congregation. Where no common thread is found, the text might be deemed irrelevant or out of date. Walter Brueggemann (2010) brought the preacher, hearers and text as actors in the sermon, proposing 'triangling' as a means of arriving at some kind of partnership in preaching. Claiming that society is now hostile to the 'scandalous' texts of Scripture, he sees danger in the earlier bidirectional, confrontational style of preaching in which the speaker simply addressed a passive congregation. In his tridirectional model, the authority of the text as a conversation partner is restored. The risk of triangling is that 'in controversies about theology and ethics ... we usually assume two parties ... pastor and people' (36). The text is either appropriated by the preacher, or silenced.

I believe that the idea of communality offers a way of involving our hearers and the Bible in what we say, and avoids both essentializing and generalizing women's experiences. I also believe that something like communality can be found in the Bible itself.

By communality I mean a commitment to allow others into community, irrespective of difference and similarity. Within the biblical tradition we find something like this back in the Old Testament. At the institution of the Passover meal (Ex. 12) God institutes a means of collective memory:

This day shall be a day of remembrance for you. You shall celebrate it as a festival to the LORD; throughout your generations you shall observe it as a perpetual ordinance. (v. 14)

Then later in Deuteronomy 26, when the offering of first fruits is instituted, we read:

When the priest takes the basket from your hand and sets it down before the altar of the LORD your God, you shall make this response before the LORD your God: 'A wandering Aramean was my ancestor; he went down into Egypt and lived there as an alien, few in number, and there he became a great nation, mighty and populous. When the Egyptians treated us harshly and afflicted us, by imposing hard labour on us, we cried to the LORD, the God of our ancestors; the LORD heard our voice and saw our affliction, our toil, and our oppression. The LORD brought us out of Egypt with a mighty hand and an outstretched arm, with a terrifying display of power, and with signs and wonders; and he brought us into this place and gave us this land, a land flowing with milk and honey. So now I bring the first of the fruit of the ground that you, O LORD, have given me.' (vv. 4–10)

There is an important change in the middle of the passage. There is a switch from the third person – a wandering Aramean was my father, he went down to Egypt, he became a great nation – to 'when the Egyptians treated *us* harshly'. First person plural – this is *our* memory, we are a people. Because God did this for *us*, *I* now bring *my* offerings. In other words, there is communality, a story shared by the people of God stretching back through time, but experienced differently by each of them. Later, Paul encouraged early churches to value unity above all. New Testament scholar N. T. Wright places at the heart of Paul's work

yearning and striving for *messianic unity across traditional boundaries*, whether it be the unity of Jew and Gentile in the Messiah (the main point of Galatians), the unity of the church under the lordship of the Messiah in a pagan and imperial context (part of the main point of Philippians, coming to memorable expression in 2.1–4), or, ... in Philemon, the unity of master and slave – communality based on an ethical commitment to place unity above difference. (Wright, 2013: 11–12)

Communality encourages the preacher to avoid reading both text and congregation for either sameness or difference, and requires us to think about how we build a welcoming space in the sermon. The task of the preacher becomes the creation of space in which, by the interaction of speaker, hearer and text, God might speak. Space-creating preaching is a different register from preaching dominated by speaker, hearers or text. It seeks not to confront, nor to instruct, but first to create space in which communality might be built. Regarding the sermon as a communal act means, for me, defining preaching first as engagement of the community in a shared story, then exploring together the biblical text that tells something of that story, and finally curating a space in which, individually and communally, the congregation might meet with God.

We are a long way now from the kind of sermon in which the preacher confronts the congregation in order to make them conform. Instead, preaching has become a kind of conversation in which all partners are involved. I do not want to dismiss preaching as a mere talking head, but I would like to suggest that preparing to preach is not a studious activity carried out in isolation. It is rather forged in the heat of communality. Sermons might begin over after-church coffee during the previous weeks, or in a home group, or as we visit others. Sharing our text with others before we preach allows them a voice in our sermon.

Narrative preaching might be best suited to including the congregation. Narratives tell stories and sustain shared cultures. They give voice to understanding gained through experience, and so liberate the women involved in the sermon, whether that be the preacher, a biblical woman or women hearers. Narrative makes space for us to reflect on how our stories interact, conflict and build on each other. Narrative can cope with tensions and surprises and contradictions, in ways that propositional preaching never can. It avoids essentialism by telling the story of 'this' woman rather than women. It can bypass the presuppositions of both speaker and hearers by telling the story of 'this' text. It allows pre-existing hegemonies to be challenged by giving alternative accounts – of coming to faith, or experiencing God, or temptation. It can avoid individualism, by using individual stories to address a shared problem. When Laura Bates embarked on her *Everyday Sexism* project (2014) she hoped that critical contributions to the debate could challenge the narrative of dominant groups. Her approach perhaps typifies how individuals can be heard, for the benefit of all: 'If I could somehow bring together all those women's stories in one place ... perhaps people would be convinced that there was ... a problem to be solved' (15). It also avoids the kind of individualism in which the preacher chooses and promotes her own canon, or where individual stories or experiences provide the filter by which biblical material can be rejected or resisted.

In the sermon that comes next, based on the woman with the issue of blood in Luke 8.40–56, I deliberately try to speak of the woman's experience, from her perspective. It is a narrative sermon in which I have been fairly free to imagine or imply some details – for example, I have assumed that at one time the woman was wealthy, because Luke tells us she spent a lot of money on doctors. I had been given the title 'Freedom from stigma', which seemed to work well with the passage.

Sermon two

At one time the woman apparently had everything. She was wealthy, healthy and accomplished. When she fell ill she had enough money to employ some good doctors. But they couldn't do anything.

Though they were happy enough to relieve her of what she had and then leave her with nothing.

Because she is a faithful member of her religious community, she worships God, she submits to the rules. Her illness makes her unclean. She is not allowed to go into the place of worship because of it. She is not allowed to mix with others because of it. When she walks down the street, if people don't get out of her way, she has to shout out 'Unclean'. From having everything she now has nothing. Not even human contact. Not even the ability to come into the presence of her God. It has all been taken away. It is as though she has become invisible.

Nobody sees her.

Nobody listens to her.

Of course, she understands that the religious leaders have no choice. They too sought to obey the law of God, and the law said that she had to be ostracized from her community and from her God.

All because she was bleeding.

After all, illness was a result of sin and even though they didn't know what this woman had done, it must have been something.

Despite everything, she hasn't quite given up. She hears about a new healer in town, who's healed all kinds of illness. She has to be careful, of course. Nobody must know that she has gone out among the villagers, she would make all of them unclean too. So she waits till the throng settles. She creeps, hunched, through the crowd of her one-time friends and neighbours, anonymous. At last, she realizes she is near to the miracle worker. She stretches out a hand and just about, at fingertip, touches his robe.

Immediately she realizes that something in her body has changed. It feels as though she has been healed.

Then – disaster.

The healer speaks, 'Who touched me?' She stays quiet. Nobody else speaks up. Peter, one of the healer's followers, tries to reason with him: 'There's a great crowd around you, it could have been anyone.' But Jesus insists: 'Power has gone out of me.'

There's nothing for it now. The woman has to step out, confess. As she stands to speak there are gasps and murmurs in the crowd – 'What's she doing here? She's made us all unclean too. That's going to cost money, for the sacrifices.' Maybe some wondered what Jesus would do – after all, he was supposed to come from God, and now an unclean woman had touched him he would have to uphold the law, send her away, go to the temple himself to be made clean again.

But Jesus sees her, and stoops to listen. Jesus does what he always does – he sees her and he hears her. Suddenly, after 12 years of rejection and ostracism she *is* someone; she matters, she is valued.

It's a remarkable enough story as it stands.

But there's more. Not only does Jesus raise this woman from living death to fullness of life, he does it before a ruler of the synagogue. One of the rulers of the synagogue who had banned this woman from their place of worship and from the community, perhaps. One of the rulers of the synagogue who had declared her unclean and said she had to isolate herself from friends and neighbours. One of the rulers of the synagogue who imposed the religious law.

He wasn't a bad man. He too realized who Jesus was. He had fallen at the feet of Jesus to beg healing for his daughter.

There isn't a bad person and a good person in this story, there are just people who need Jesus, and people Jesus cares for.

But Jairus was also probably a child of his time. He was important, the woman was not. His daughter was not yet at the age of responsibility, so her illness was not the result of sin. The woman was adult and must have brought her condition on herself. He had banished the woman from society and yet here she was among the crowd. His daughter's life was ahead of her, the woman had had her life. There were many reasons why Jesus should deal with the woman quickly and get on to Jairus' daughter.

But Jesus takes his time.

And when he has finished, someone comes to tell Jairus that his daughter is dead.

Although Jesus had stopped for the woman, he is not diverted by bad news. He carries on to Jairus' house. 'She isn't dead, just sleeping,' he tells the family. They mock him. But he carries on, takes the girl by the hand and raises the girl to life.

It's easy in this story to head straight for the miracles – Jesus heals the woman and raises the girl to life, end of.

But there is so much more to it than that. Jesus stops on his way to the home of an important person to spend time with, to listen to, an insignificant woman. Jesus overturns the religious law – twice in the same story he is touched by what is unclean and does not recoil. Jesus' progress towards the girl is apparently delayed but it is never deflected. He does things in his own time.

From the woman's point of view he doesn't simply fix her, he heals her. The years of rejection are redeemed by his seeing her. The ostracism is overcome for she is publicly healed by someone at whose feet the synagogue leader has just knelt. Community itself is restored.

Jesus not only heals those who are labelled unclean – the woman with the haemorrhage and the dead girl – he restores those who have rejected them too. Imagine what Jairus learns – a leader who ostracized the woman because of something she could not help. Or the crowd who once were her friends but who submitted to social and religious pressure and rejected her. Jesus does not only restore the woman physically but spiritually and socially too – he listens to her story.

And we are in this story too, you and I. Perhaps as the weak and insignificant. Perhaps as the one who imposes the rules. Perhaps as an onlooker. Jesus sees us too.

I don't know whether you watched the BBC drama *Apple Tree Yard* recently. I found it very disturbing. But the explanation for all that happens to Yvonne seems to me to be contained in three words, 'you saw me'. Despite her professional success and financial security, Yvonne had felt invisible. When somebody sees her, really sees her, it feels like water on a parched land.

We all want to be seen, and we are able to see others. It's a theme in Luke's Gospel that Jesus both sees people and tells others to do so. Jairus and the other synagogue leaders had not seen the woman, they had seen the law and the illness. When community is fractured that's what happens. We don't see people, we see something about them, or something about us that we want to protect. With Jesus there is no stigma, no uncleanness, no rejection. He sees each person, and he asks us to do the same.

To see the person others exclude. To see the insignificant or unimportant. To see those with whom we disagree. To see even ourselves, as we really are.

And perhaps more challengingly, as Jesus saw the marginalized woman and the dead girl, and even the important man, so he sees you and he sees me. He sees where we are weak and where we are strong.

Sometimes it feels like we can't do anything to make the world a better place.

Actually, we can do almost everything that is needed to bring the presence of God to the people we meet. It just involves seeing them.

Time for reflection

In this reflection you are invited to think about your faith development and how it influences what you say in sermons.

My faith journey

Think about your own faith journey. *What part did relationship and connectedness play? Does the way you preach or lead emphasize the importance of connection? What might 'communality' mean for your preaching if you were to adopt it as a principle?*

Read this poem by Nicola Slee and *pray about how you might support women you know*:

I do not stand alone
But with others to support me
I will stand my ground.

I do not see the way
But with others to walk it with me
I can make a path.

I do not possess the truth
But with others to witness to what they know
I will be able to discern what is right.

I cannot master all skills
But with others who will lend their accomplishments
I can do enough.

I cannot carry every burden
But with others to share it
I may bear my own load.

I cannot meet all needs
But with others to nourish and replenish me
I will be able to give enough.

I do not have limitless free choice
But with others to consult
I will make my own choices gladly.

I will not always be consistent
But with others to laugh with me
I will regain my equanimity.

I am not invincible
But with others to reach out a hand
I may learn from my mistakes and start again.

I cannot be perfect
But with others to make up the shortfall of my imperfections
I can be content to be good enough.

© Nicola Slee (2004)

Notes

1 Census, 2011.

2 Wellard, S. (2011). *Doing it All? Grandparents, childcare and employment: An Analysis of British Social Attitudes Survey.*

3 Domestic Abuse in England and Wales, Full fact, the UK's independent factchecking charity, 2018.

5

Hearing Bible Women

I have offered three basic approaches to Bible reading open to women preachers: rejection, repatriation and redemption. The choice depends to a large extent on how our experience interacts with our theology. For me, experience has sent me back over and again to question my biblical interpretation. Sometimes my understanding of the Bible has changed, sometimes my understanding of experience. I would not want to reject the Bible. It is central to Christian preaching. Without it we might give good motivational speeches, or helpful spiritual reflections, but we will not be preaching. Sometimes repatriation offers new insights by placing the text in its original setting. It can be a first step towards redeeming or reclaiming it. As women preachers we need to be acutely aware of which strategy we are using, and why we have chosen to do so. Helpful strategies start with becoming aware of my own position and experience, alongside what tradition and culture might tell us.

Reflecting on Bible women

Earlier I identified four standpoints which are useful in approaching biblical passages – culture, tradition, experience and position. Culture might mean the culture at the time of the story, the culture of the writer or that of the reader. Tradition can mean what the Bible itself seems to say, or how it has been interpreted through church history. Experience and position relate to 'me', whether I have experienced something like what happens in the text, or have experience of the text in some way, and what I believe about what the text seems to say.

Let's examine the person of Mary, the mother of Jesus, using these four sources. In this kind of reflection it is possible to start with any of the four perspectives, and they do overlap in places. I will start here with Position and then move on to Tradition – what the Bible says and how it has been interpreted over time.

Position

My personal position is that the Bible itself is not sexist. I can say that partly because I do not believe that the Bible itself is anything. Each book and writer has something different to say. Each of them reflects the hegemonies of the time, which were almost entirely patriarchal. These writings have been interpreted by a male normative Church, and where they challenge the status quo women have been intentionally written out, as happened, for example, with the apostle Junia. Paul mentions Junia in Romans 16.7. The NRSV says: 'Greet Andronicus and Junia, my relatives who were in prison with me; they are prominent among the apostles, and they were in Christ before I was.' Junia was a fairly well known woman's name – there are around 250 examples of it in Greek and Latin inscriptions found in Rome alone. Yet, over time, Junia became Junias – a masculinized version of the name for which there is no evidence. The process of interpretation was probably influenced by the underlying narrative of the translators that 'a woman couldn't have been an apostle'. As Bird says in his recent commentary on Romans (2016: 6):

> There is a tsunami of textual and patristic evidence for 'Junia' that proves overwhelming. Despite some naughty scribes, biased translators, lazy lexicographers and dogmatic commentators, the text speaks about a woman named 'Junia'.

Elsewhere the transformation of Junia into the masculine Junias is referred to as a 'figment of chauvinistic imagination'.

Second, my position is that as women readers and interpreters of the Bible it is our task to read between the lines, and to find the women. The Bible needs to be recovered for women. As a result, when I come to read about Mary, I want to find a woman not an icon, someone with whom I, and other women, can identify.

Tradition

For many Christians down through history, Mary is the model of what a true woman ought to be. She is in the story as an incubator and nurturer of life, subsequently silenced and subservient. I recently asked a young woman in my church which Bible women she was familiar with. Almost inevitably she mentioned 'lots of Marys', especially the 'prostitute one' and the 'mother of Jesus'. 'Would you like to be like any of them?' I asked. 'Certainly not Jesus' mother,' she replied. 'She was too dependent on Joseph.'

Mary is introduced in patriarchal fashion, precedence is given to her condition and her relationship to a man, rather than her name. She is a virgin pledged to be married. Despite the patriarchal introduction, what Luke says next must have immediately jarred with the assumptions of his early readers. It is this insignificant woman to whom an angel has been sent, and the message is given, 'favoured one! The Lord is with you.' In what way could this woman be favoured? Traditionally it has often been assumed that the favour is about to be bestowed, the conception of the Son of God. Yet this is not necessarily the case. Raymond Brown, in his classic work (1999: 634), writes, 'I do *not* think that in Luke's mind the only grace Mary received was to be mother of God's son ... Mary was already looked on by God with favour.' Brown suggests no evidence for this view, simply that 'God's plans are long in existence.' Although the angel does tell Mary that she has 'found favour with God', precisely why and how remain unclear. Others, by contrast, consider that Luke's intention is to emphasize Mary's unworthiness, perhaps to emphasize God's incarnation into a generally unworthy world. From the story itself we know only that at the point in time when the angel greets Mary she *is* blessed and the Lord *is* with her.

Over the years Mary has been rendered either so transcendent that we cannot speak of her in concrete, human terms or so subservient that her model is damaging to women, as my young friend indicated. In some quarters her state at the time of conception (virgin or otherwise) has been made a litmus test of true faith. Despite all this she is portrayed by Luke as a very human young woman. Although in art she is often portrayed at her prie-dieu when the angel appears, there is no indication in the text that she is doing anything other than getting on with everyday life.

Luke's transition from one age to the next, as portrayed in his early chapters, offers fertile ground for women preachers. His first story (Luke 1) deals with an announcement to a priest (the 'right' person), in the temple (the 'right' place), whose hope of a child must be gone; a story that perhaps recalls the first covenant between God and Abraham. By contrast, the new covenant comes into being through a young woman who is not in the temple at the time of the announcement, but in a place to which no Old Testament expectation is attached. This contrast introduces a typically Lucan theme present in both the Gospel and Acts, the 'sacred' space for the inclusive people of God. What God traditionally did, and does again, in the temple, he will now do in the household, the new sacred space.

What follows now stems still from the source of Tradition, but is more clearly influenced by my own position.

Position

By having the pregnant Mary, in the Magnificat, identify God as her Saviour, Luke associates salvation, the definitive act by which God keeps God's promise to Israel and ultimately reveals God's mercy, with the birth of Jesus. The tenses in the Magnificat (God '*has* helped his servant Israel', 'My spirit rejoices in God my Saviour') are awkward if salvation is linked to Jesus' death, but make sense if salvation began with the conception of the Messiah. If that is the moment of God's intervention, Mary can indeed announce the new commonwealth.

To move the moment of salvation from the death of Jesus to his conception, as appears to be indicated by Mary's Magnificat, has some significant implications. Feminist theologians have often correctly accused Christianity of an obsession with suffering and death, because of its focus on the suffering Christ. Affliction has been almost glamorized, and hardship has gained a spiritual mystique. This thinking implies a number of problems: first, it can lead to the normalization, even glorification, of suffering. Rather than wanting to help the poor, protest their suffering, militate against their exploitation, Christians have too often professed envy of them: 'It's so much easier to believe in God when that's all you have.' For women this has particular problems, for poverty does have a woman's face. Second, it validates violence as a means to an end. Language about violence in war, for example, generally justifies violence as having a higher purpose. Again, this is problematic for women, because women suffer most of the world's violence.

Elaine Storkey highlights this in *Scars Across Humanity*:

> Violence against women has actually been celebrated in dance and traditional rituals; it has been glorified in art, literature, film and music. In the history of even Western culture, male aggression has been described or depicted without censor, and women's suffering re-presented as somehow beautiful or part of her journey to refinement. (2015: 16)

It is not difficult to see how a patriarchal narrative accommodates the glorification of suffering as seen in some traditional accounts of the gospel, and how this, in turn, assists the suppression of women. If, however, the key moment of God's saving intervention is at conception, the focus of salvation becomes not the death of Christ, but the life of God in Christ. The contrast between the old and new ages becomes even starker if the salvific moment is that moment of conception, for Mary becomes in some senses the ark of the new covenant. The sense of the narrative, that Mary is overshadowed by the Holy Spirit, becomes pregnant, announces the new commonwealth in terms of what God has already done, and gives birth to a child whom the shepherds are told is the Saviour, implies that Mary carries the presence of God until the time to give birth arrives. This interpretation gives Mary a more significant role in the plan of salvation than simply being an incubator for the Christ-child.

This view also addresses the problem of the abusive God, maltreating God's people and God's Son, Jesus. If salvation comes at conception, through life, when God becomes irrevocably involved with the world, the abused God need not be the focus of adulation, nor interpreted as legitimate abuse. If God's primary intervention is at conception, then the suffering of Jesus comes at the instigation of humankind, rather than at the hands of a cruel Father. In addition, where our notion of God is transcendent and perhaps dispassionate, the birth of Jesus implies immanence and presence.

Culture

How might reflection on the culture of the time guide our thinking? It would be entirely consistent with the times for Mary to have been raped, some suggest. That kind of idea arouses much anger. Whether it is theological or cultural anger remains a moot point. The redemptive activity of God in such a scenario would be obvious. Objections surround the incarnate nature of Jesus if he had been conceived in the usual way, and the purity of Mary if she were simply a young woman, rather than a virgin. However we interpret the start of the story, there seems to be unworthiness in humanity, favour shown to Mary, and through her to the rest of the world, and a God who looks in favour on people.

Mary is a westernized rendering of the Old Testament name Mariam, which recalls Mary's fore-sister Miriam, the one who, alongside Moses and Aaron, led God's people out of captivity in Egypt. Her history and culture tell her about God's dealings with people; her name links her to one who led people out of slavery. Perhaps among her prayers is a request that her people be freed from Roman rule. Perhaps, as well as historic and cultural faith, she has a personal faith in the God of her ancestors. She does seem to understand who the angel is, at least. And her knowledge of her people's history would also tell her that God's dealings with people can be demanding and hard. She may even have been made conscious, as she matured, of the person who shared her name and led Israel to freedom. If so, her expectation of women would not be meekness and mildness. Is it possible that, far from the angel appearing to a subservient, self-effacing young woman, God's call in fact goes to a woman who is strong in character and eager to see God act as God had done in the past?

I was recently working with a group of women analysing the outcome of some research I had done. Listening to their conversations was fascinating. After over an hour of discussion about what it means to be a woman preacher and how to encourage women preachers, one woman said, 'But it isn't only about us, is it? We need to be inclusive.' The language of the group changed for a while and they began to speak about 'everyone' and 'all'. Then, tentatively, one woman spoke up: 'We're writing ourselves out of this, aren't we? I mean, by including everyone, the women's voices have disappeared.' It was an example of a more famous story recounted by Elisabeth Moltmann-Wendel of a religious gathering in Nicaragua. People had met together to read Bible passages and then discuss their meaning. On reading the story of Easter morning, the peasant women got very excited, seeing themselves in the passage. 'Women are braver than men', 'women have more heart', they said. But gradually, in a microcosm of history, the men won back the ground – 'It wasn't as dangerous for the women as it was for the men to be at the tomb.' A compromise was reached – 'The women played an important role as did the men.' But effectively, *her-story* was rewritten.

This rewriting has happened to Mary. Her story has been subsumed in a patriarchal canon and masculinized theology in which she must be pure and meek and subservient. It is as though Luke's traditional introduction of her as a 'virgin engaged to a man' is not followed up by his story of her surprising encounter with a messenger of God while going about her daily business. Mary has much to teach us if we read her properly. She is strong and wise; she shows courage in accepting her challenge; and she understands something of collaborative faithful living – the significant tension between personal discipleship and the activity of God. Without God, Mary could not bring the Messiah into the world. Without Mary, God would not.

During her pregnancy, Mary goes to visit her cousin Elizabeth. Whether she was escaping suspicious glances and seeking solace with a relative, or not, we don't know. It is perhaps this part of the story that leads to the image of Mary as meek and subservient, bowing to social pressure and running away. But there is more to it than that. Companionship was, and is, a feature of Middle Eastern culture. Mary travels to accompany Elizabeth, and perhaps to be accompanied by her. The relationship between the women is significant, for Elizabeth's proclamation releases Mary into powerful prophecy. The relationship between the women models a new kind of kingdom, in which God is revealed in community and disciples are interdependent; a prophetic communality which recognizes their need of one another, and for collaboration if God's commonwealth is to come. It is the kind of relationship women might be well placed to model, and that is well appreciated. Feedback from a Women's Voices conference at which the then Bishop of Stockport, Libby Lane, and I both spoke, commented on how much our 'collaborative friendship' meant to those in attendance.

Frequently, particularly in evangelical churches (based on

my own experience), the story of Mary is lost from Advent and Christmas as we focus on the incarnation and coming of Emmanuel. We lose it at the peril of women, however. The meeting of Elizabeth and Mary can be seen as the crux of Luke's transition narrative from Israel's story to the story of Jesus, represented by an ageing barren wife and an expectant virgin – two marginalized women. The new era is brought about through a new creation, wrought in the body of a woman. As Elizabeth greets Mary, proclaims God's blessing over her and the child she is carrying, and recognizes her status as 'the mother of my Lord', Mary is released into prophesying the new commonwealth. The announcement of the new commonwealth does not come out of the power or splendour of the temple, but out of the prophetic communality of two women in a home, the new sacred space and a new prophetic relationship.

The story recounted by Luke includes Elizabeth feeling the baby in her womb kick, and Mary visiting the temple for purification after the birth of Jesus. The narrative is low on detail, but clearly relates to women's bodily experiences. Our culture, however, based on Greek thought, regards the material world as inferior to the spiritual, and so the annual recounting of the nativity makes little comment on the physicality or vulnerability or intense humanity of birth, and says even less about the fact that Jesus was an embodied, gendered self, born of a woman.

Experience

While it is certainly true that I have had no experiences akin to those of Mary's meeting with the angel, or birthing the Son of God, I do have experience that might be fruitful in other ways. In particular, I want to think about the meeting, and implied relationship, between Mary and Elizabeth.

I remember as a young person in the church feeling the kind of pity for Elizabeth that I might feel for someone who came second in an exam or a competition. I saw her then as someone who had put up with years of barrenness and the judgements that would incite in the culture of the time, who was finally lulled into thinking she had 'made it', only to be told that actually she came second. It's a naive rendering of the story, certainly. But it does lead to some useful insights.

Sermon snippet

The meeting between Elizabeth and Mary is significant. Where we might naturally find tension, there is none. Elizabeth has waited decades for a child, probably even given up praying for one. At last, miraculously, God promises her a son who will be special, who will bring joy to many, be great before the Lord and announce the commonwealth of God – the special son of worthy parents. Then, just as Elizabeth is revelling in the delight of being pregnant, enjoying the respect of her neighbours, so long denied to her as a barren woman, her cousin arrives – young, unmarried, pregnant. Elizabeth could have been resentful. She could have felt her new-found position usurped by Mary. She could have turned her away. Yet she does none of those things. She acknowledges the situation: 'Why am I so favoured, that the mother of my Lord should come to me?' And this recognition of Mary and the baby she carries releases the announcement of the commonwealth of God in Mary's Magnificat.

Mary receives from Elizabeth a companionship which releases her prophecy of the new commonwealth. It accompanies her as she faces the challenges implicit in the work of God in her. Neither woman controls the situation; both are obedient to God and supportive of each other. This kind of companionship, allowing God to do his work in the other person while simply keeping them company, a kind of midwife role, resonates through Luke's story of Mary.

In the enabling company of Elizabeth, in response to her affirmation of the activity of God, Mary announces the new commonwealth, exercising a prophetic ministry which serves as a model for women articulating a new vision of God's reign. The Magnificat

---

announces not only the end of patriarchy, 'From now on all generations will call me (a woman) blessed', but an end to all hierarchical structures. Mary heralds a threefold revolution that favours the oppressed, allows them good things and gives them access to power.

Announcing a new commonwealth

Just as Mary announced good news for the oppressed, so should we. Just as she declared the voiceless now have access to power, so can we. A key issue for women preachers, I believe, is not gender equality, but gender justice. A powerful way of working for justice is to speak out from the perspective of the oppressed. The dominance of men in the patriarchal narrative is not explicitly promoted. It doesn't need to be. Images of men dominate in almost all aspects of life. Take, for example, money. Of all the denominations of bank notes used in Britain, other than the Queen, only one bears the face of a woman – and it took someone to notice their absence. In 2015 the Bank of England announced that Winston Churchill would appear on new £5 notes, replacing Elizabeth Fry. Caroline Criado Perez noticed, and launched a campaign that resulted in Jane Austen appearing on £10 notes. Without someone noticing we would deal with money that uniquely represented male images. It matters, because girls and women need to see their gender represented in everyday ways in images of authority. It is thoughtless, everyday sexism that results in women being largely represented as victims (in British media 79 per cent of victims are women, while 75 per cent of 'experts' are men).[1]

A similar thing happens when we read the Bible. Women can be airbrushed out, and their stories ignored. Announcing the commonwealth of God involves reading the Bible from liminal spaces, and retelling the story.

During a series on Judges, I was given the opportunity to speak on Judges 19, the story of the Levite's concubine. The point of the story, I was assured by colleagues, was that there was no king in the land (no male authority figure). It was, according to them, a story about what happens when there is no strong leadership. The woman, apparently, was incidental.

Sermon

The minibus taking Helen and me into Bwaise couldn't go any farther. Even the normally rough and muddy Ugandan road had given out. So we began the walk down towards the railway line. It was a sunny Ugandan day. At the top of the hill men sat round upturned oil drums, playing cards, gambling and drinking. If this was the slums, it didn't look too bad. But as we went downhill the smell got worse, the flies got more persistent and we – I should say I – began to notice the sewage backing up along the side of the road.

At the bottom of the hill were the women. I hadn't seen any up to that point. They were scavenging for food, using the water by the railway line to wash and looking after beautiful but flea-ridden children. The difference between the women's experience of poverty and the men's could not have been more different.

There's something of that difference in the story we had read.

At first sight, the story is an episode in a love story. The concubine leaves her man. This story was so little known among Christians that when I mentioned it to a very biblically literate friend, she admitted she had never come across it before.

In Israel being a concubine was respectable. It was not the same as marriage, but not unlike it either, although the concubine was of lower status than the wife. What is clear is that the status of the woman is defined in terms of her sexual relationship to a man. As with many love stories, once the woman has gone, the man decides he wants her back. He goes to her father's house to find her, and so keen is he to win her back that he spends his time drinking and eating with his father-in-law and doesn't seem to speak to the concubine at all. Eventually, he leaves with her.

Rather than take the advice of his servant about how far they can get before nightfall, the Levite rejects the idea of staying in Jerusalem – which was not an Israelite town at the time – and decides to head for Gibeah or Ramah. Ultimately, the man's xenophobia has a horrible irony about it.

In Gibeah they meet an old man who advises them not to spend the night in the town square because Gibeah is a rough town. He takes them in, but the men of Gibeah try to get him to send the Levite out to them so they can rape him. The man refuses them his male guest, but offers his virgin daughter and the Levite's concubine. The woman is pushed out by her own man, and gang raped all night. The next morning the Levite finds her dying on the doorstep. He bundles her up on to his donkey and goes home, where he butchers her body and sends a piece to each of the tribes of Israel. Cutting up her body and denying her burial could be seen as even worse than the rape, because in Israel not to be buried was the worst fate possible.

The tribes of Israel begin a war against Gibeah to punish them. Forty thousand Israelites die, and 25,000 Benjaminites (Gibeah was from the tribe of Benjamin) die in battle and Gibeah is overrun. Because the Israelites have sworn not to marry their daughters to Benjaminite men there is a danger the tribe of Benjamin will die out. They find a town that did not swear the oath and kill everyone in the town apart from 400 virgins who are married off to the remaining Benjaminites. Any Benjaminite who does not get a wife this way is encouraged to watch the girls of Shiloh when they come out to dance at a festival and to perform what is commonly called marriage by rape.

How on earth did this story make it into the Bible? It's appalling!

The story tells us exactly what it's like to be powerless. Despite the fact that the Levite apparently sets out to woo the woman back, he ends up carousing with her father, and none of the story is told from the woman's point of view. Probably she had no choice as to whether or not to return. When her father had partied sufficiently with the Levite he may just have pushed her out the door. Similarly, she has no say in where to spend the night. And the old man rescuer was interested only in saving the man.

In fact, if we look at what the man actually says, he describes the rape of another man as a 'vile act' and prevents it. But in handing over the women, he tells the gang to do what is 'good in their eyes'. Even the wicked men are allowed to do what is good in their eyes, including the violation of women.

The first time the Levite, who had set out to woo back his concubine, actually speaks to her is in the morning, when he tells the dying woman to get up and move.

What is so awful about this story?

The writer makes no comment about the behaviour of any of those involved.

There is a significant contrast between this story and that of Abraham and Isaac. When Abraham takes the knife to kill Isaac, God intervenes. When the Levite takes the knife to kill the concubine even God remains silent. Nobody defends this woman from gang rape. Nobody speaks up when the Levite puts her on his donkey to return her home, and there hacks her into twelve pieces. In the face of such suffering, God, and the narrator, is silent.

How do such things happen?

At the Greenbelt festival one year, I went to hear a Christian Aid speaker on the topic of 'Putting Women in their Place'. It was a very full session. On the way out my husband realized he had left something under his seat, and I waited at the door while he retrieved it. I noticed a very profound thing. Most of the younger people came out promising never to forget what they had heard, they wanted to get involved. In general, middle-aged women came out silent, stunned. But this was the remarkable and worrying thing. Many middle-aged men came out saying things like, 'You don't know how reliable the statistics are', or 'I think that was a bit over the top.' In other words, looking for reasons to be silent. I am not against men. The issue is not that these were men, but that in the face of evidence about the treatment of women now, in the twenty-first century, the reaction of some people was to look for reasons to keep silent.

Let me share some of those statistics with you:

In the UK 230 women a day are raped; two women a week are killed by a present or former partner; one woman is assaulted in her own home every six seconds; 45 per cent of women have experienced some form of domestic violence, sexual assault or stalking.

Globally, of the 1.4 billion people living in poverty, 70 per cent are women; 1 in 3 women has been beaten, coerced into sex or abused; between 200,000 and 300,000 women are trafficked into Europe every year.

And yet, even here, I suspect that what I say is being heard not as a plea on behalf of the marginalized, poor and abused, but as feminist rhetoric. And the Church spends more time talking about whether women should be bishops, or allowed to lead or preach, than it does seeking justice.

The story in the Bible is horrendous, because when some powerful human beings are allowed to set an agenda that reduces other human beings to commodities to be traded, or sub-humans to be abused, the results are horrendous.

Why did God not speak? Why does God not speak?

I have no easy answers. But I want to suggest that God works through people, and that God's people are selective about what they will do. Just as the old man offered protection to the Levite, but sent out the women to be abused, so we too make choices.

It is often said by those outside the Church that our job is to make Christian comment and not to get involved politically. People are happy for the Church to offer charity, but not to question why charity is needed. We can host foodbanks, but not lobby MPs.

Even within the Church we have made God a God of charity and kindness, and ignored prophets like Amos who said 'let justice roll down like waters'; or Micah who asked, 'what does the Lord require of you but to do justice, and to love kindness, and to walk humbly with your God?'; or Isaiah, 'learn to do good; seek justice.'

The fight for justice begins when somebody recognizes something is wrong. When we don't hide from it, or find an excuse to ignore it, but when we stand up and say 'that's wrong'.

It is not power that corrupts but fear. Fear of losing power corrupts those who wield it and fear of the scourge of power corrupts those who are subject to it.

Back to our story of the Levite and the concubine. Society allows this abuse to happen – the men of Gibeah are invited to do with the women what is right in their own eyes; the men are defended. The Levite is so affronted that his concubine has been abused he chops her up and sends her bits to the tribes of Israel. War and more death ensue. To avert the risk of the tribe of Benjamin dying out, more women are abused and rape is again condoned. How does it happen?

Nobody stands up for justice for all, only justice for the powerful.

Even God is silent.

Why do we have this story?

Because it challenges.

What will we do, you and I, in the face of injustice?

Robert F. Kennedy said this in 1966:

It is from numberless diverse acts of courage and belief that human history is shaped. Each time [someone] stands up for an ideal, or acts to improve the lot of others, or strikes out against injustice, [they] send forth a tiny ripple of hope, and crossing each other from a million different centres of energy and daring, those ripples build a current which can sweep down the mightiest walls of oppression and resistance.

It's the little things. Imagine if the Levite had simply gone to woo his concubine, and then gone home; or if he had listened to his servant instead of his prejudice and spent the night in Jerusalem; or if the old man had simply barred the door until the men of Gibeah had sobered up.

Little things make a big difference. It doesn't take much to raise our eyes above our home groups, our parishes, our Bible study and see opportunities to fight for justice – use online petitions from Tearfund or Christian Aid; write to our MPs; ask questions when elections come round.

When we ignore matters of justice, people die.

Strategies for hearing Bible women

Why do we need women to read and preach the Bible as women? First, because, for hundreds of years it has been interpreted only through the lens of male experience. It is not that women have not been included, the problem goes beyond that. Centuries of male-centric biblical interpretation have resulted in man's experience becoming human experience/human experience becoming man's experience. 'Man' is neutral, whereas 'woman' is freighted with problems. In biblical interpretation, the word 'man' may have originally been gender neutral, but its neutrality has been lost. In the Genesis story, Adam, over time, has become distinctly man. Eve, the woman, tempted him and he fell, therefore woman has been blamed for the fall of man. Despite the fact that Adam originally meant 'earthling' – a generic human, not man, generations of women have been defined in light of this story.

Of particular concern for women preachers, I believe, is the fact that the normalizing of 'male' has completely eclipsed women's experiences from biblical interpretation. Man's experiences and understandings have become canonized, women's have been eliminated. Not only do successive generations not hear their experiences spoken of, but they increasingly lack the language with which to speak of them. When only men's voices are heard, the Bible begins to support patriarchy. Women's voices can be excluded, because they are not present in the first place. Women become so far removed from biblical tradition that they are not included in it. And because we are not included, we are regarded not as part of the biblical story but as an anomaly, unworthy of serious consideration simply because we are not men. The first step in fighting injustice is always to notice it then to reveal it. The first reaction against this revelation is to re-hide the truth. Hence the most powerful kickback against campaigns such as #MeToo is not to refute, but simply to claim that 'it has gone too far'.

As I said in Chapter 3, we have to tell the truth about sexism if we are to stand against it.

So, how do we spot when the Bible seems to be offering up women as convenient scapegoats and interpret it differently?

When it comes to exegesis, I ask myself three simple questions:

- Where is the power?
- What's on the page?
- What's the underlying story?

Where's the power?

When I offered a group of students an alternative interpretation of Bathsheba's story in 2 Samuel 11, suggesting that Bathsheba had been raped, a number of men objected strongly. Several women, on the other hand, were vocally supportive. My interpretation came not from a close reading of the text, although that does support my premise, but from asking the question 'Where's the power?' The basics of the story are clear: David sees a woman, David sends someone to fetch her, David lies with her and sends her home; Bathsheba conceives and lets David know she is pregnant. Conception is not a voluntary activity, in the way that seeing, sending for, lying with and sending away are. Bathsheba exercises subjectivity only when she sends to tell David she is pregnant.

Looking for the power can yield some interesting interpretations. Reread the story of Paul and his companions in Philippi, for example (Acts 16.16–40). The story begins with a demon-possessed slave girl following the apostle around and, basically, getting on his nerves. Matthew Henry suggests: 'It is observable how subtle Satan is, that great tempter, in taking the opportunity to give us diversion when we are going about any religious exercises.' Note the influence of centuries of male-dominated Bible interpretation – the girl is no more than a distraction! Considered from a Christian perspective, however, where is the power? Surely it is with the apostles.

Sermon snippet

On first reading it might seem like these early Christians, as they walk through the streets of Philippi, demonstrate power over an evil spirit, then put up with beating and imprisonment, and yet still praise God.

And we might think, 'What a great story. Why can't we see opportunities for mission like that?'

Let's look at it again.

Paul, Silas and Luke are preoccupied with the business of religion. They are on their way to church when this girl starts shouting after them. They are so preoccupied in fact that they fail to see, fail to *really* see, their mission to the city. They are so busy going about the *busy*-ness of faith that they forget what really is the *business* of faith. In fact, the way Luke tells the story (and Luke is a big Paul fan), Paul only sets the girl free because she is getting on his nerves. I wonder if the fact that neither he nor his companions do anything to help straight away is because they don't really see this girl. She is, after all, a slave, demon-possessed and a nuisance. Yet she is innocent. She is not to blame for her enslavement, nor her possession, and she is being a nuisance by telling the truth – the absolute truth: these men are servants of the Most High God. Yet Paul frees her because she is getting on his nerves.

For a while the great apostle Paul seems to have lost focus on his mission. He is concentrating on getting to prayer rather than on bringing the commonwealth of God to the town where he was.

Once he remembers that the job of a follower of Jesus is to bring freedom to the captives, he is focused.

What's on the page?

In the David and Bathsheba story the insight gained from watching the power dynamics is confirmed by what is on the page. The Bible implies that Bathsheba was religiously faithful, and that she had every right to be on the roof, because verse

4 tells us: 'Now she was purifying herself after her period.'
Menstruation, *niddah*, is unclean in the Old Testament (and
for some Christians now, for example the person who asked a
woman priest to inform them when she was on her period, so
they wouldn't take communion from her). After it the Jewish
law required the woman to completely immerse herself in the
waters of *mikvah*, with nothing between the water and her
body – she had to be naked. The waters of *mikvah* had to be
gathered naturally, which meant they had to be collected rainwater. The best place to collect rainwater? The roof. Bathsheba
was there for religious reasons.

What do we find 'on the page' concerning Paul's visit to
Philippi?

First, Paul does not go to the synagogue, there isn't one. He
finds Lydia and her household at a place of prayer. In the context of the story, and the culture of the time, Paul encountered
real oppression in Philippi. The garment trade, then as now,
was not greatly revered, and the task of dyeing purple was
unpleasant. Perhaps in Lydia's household Paul observed first-
hand the effects of economic disadvantage. Later, the girl who
proclaimed the truth so loudly was a slave, a mere possession.
Maybe Paul appreciated what that meant by meeting her.
Certainly, he allowed himself, and his companions, to be
beaten and thrown in jail, thus identifying with the oppressed.

But in Philippi, Paul uses two strategies. He identifies with
the oppressed in their suffering, but he also claims equality with
those in power, by declaring his Roman citizenship. In Philippi
citizenship was a big deal. In 42 BCE this was the place where
Mark Antony and Octavian defeated Brutus and Cassius,
the people who assassinated Julius Caesar. It was a pleasant
location, and veterans of the victorious army were settled there.
Philippi became a luxury resort for former soldiers who had
the privilege of Roman citizenship conferred upon them. By
claiming his Roman citizenship, Paul was claiming equal status
with those who had beaten him. He both identifies with the
oppressed and demands the right to speak to their oppressors.

What's the underlying story?

As far as David and Bathsheba are concerned, the underlying story is that of David, the man after God's own heart (1 Sam. 13.14). David is a Christian hero, the boy who slew a giant, the king who conquered Jerusalem, the ruler who brought Israel together, the ancestor of Jesus. As a result, those he damaged are incidental to the story, particularly if they are women. Including her-story in the tale of David changes it profoundly. He is no longer a man entirely after God's own heart. Rather, he betrays his God when expedient. His self-centredness leads to disaster for daughter, wife and son. The story underlying the tradition of David falls apart when examined in the light of the one behind the biblical person.

Similarly the tradition that sees Paul as single-mindedly missional seems to underpin the view that he cared little for social justice, and less for women. This is to misread Paul. Paul speaks of the gospel almost entirely in the language of justice (Rom. 3.26: 'he himself is righteous and that he justifies the one who has faith in Jesus'). Of course, he cannot be reconstructed as simply as that. Paul has provided the bases on which patriarchal, female-excluding narratives have been built for centuries. I cannot rehabilitate the apostle here, but it is worth considering the levels of seriousness attached to two of Paul's sayings in certain spheres of the Church:

1 Corinthians 14.34–35
women should be silent in the churches. For they are not permitted to speak, but should be subordinate, as the law also says. If there is anything they desire to know, let them ask their husbands at home. For it is shameful for a woman to speak in church.

Galatians 3.28
There is no longer Jew or Greek, there is no longer slave or free, there is no longer male and female; for all of you are one in Christ Jesus.

And second, let me tentatively suggest, not as a biblical scholar, but as someone who reads and loves the Bible, that we understand Paul wrongly because of the position of his epistles in the New Testament. Working with ministry students over the last ten years I am keenly aware that many churches and Christians treat Paul as the person who explains the Gospels, as though Matthew, Mark, Luke and John were written first and then Paul explained them to the churches he founded during his missionary journeys. Actually, the Gospels were written *after* Paul. Supposing, speculatively, that the Gospel writers, who had heard reliable stories of Jesus, particularly his dealings with women, heard what Paul had to say and wanted to correct it in some way. After all, where Paul seems to tell women to be quiet, Jesus stoops to hear them speak! If there were even a grain of truth in that proposition, our ideas of the New Testament and what it says about women would change radically.

Time for Reflection

This reflection focuses on Bible women, and how we might get to know them better.

'Anyone who loves the biblical Mary Magdalene, and compares her with the "Christian" Mary Magdalene, must get very angry' (Moltmann-Wendel, 1982: 64). This is part of a liturgy published by Churches Together in Britain and Ireland and written by Nicola Slee (2001):

We denounce the hateful names they called you:
Prostitute, Whore, Harlot;
Temptress, Sinner, Slut.
...
We renounce the pernicious images they painted of you:
Voluptuous, sensuous, curvaceous,
Every straight man's best sexual fantasy.
...

We reclaim the names with which
they should have honoured you:
Woman of noble stature,
woman of upright life,
woman of bold countenance and bearing.
Woman of means, woman of substance,
providing out of your largesse for Jesus and his companions.

If you have a favourite Bible women, how could you reclaim her life? *What attracts you to her? What do you dislike about her? You could write a letter to her, or imagine her alongside you as you pray.*

Note

1 Research on thewomansroom.org.uk

6

Sermons for Women

We have now thought about why women preachers might intentionally preach as women, and what we have to offer to our congregations. I have also, I hope, explored the kind of culture in which we live, and why we might want to critique it. I have suggested that we need a clear model of maturity and discipleship that includes women's experience. I have talked about avoiding generalizations by engaging with the lives of biblical women and bearing our own testimony. I have expressed the view that being transformed might well mean enabling women to think more rather than less of ourselves. We have also thought about communality and what that might mean.

Maturity: letting Mary grow up

Mary the mother of Jesus has largely been airbrushed out of our preaching. In Reformed theology she is presented simply as *theotokos*, the 'God bearer', an obedient young girl who does as God asks, and more or less disappears once Jesus is born. In more Catholic theology she is venerated for her purity and vulnerability, but remains an eternal virgin. There is, I think, more to Mary than either of those positions. Women, I believe, need a grown-up Mary.

Sermon snippet

I was texting a friend the other day about running – we've both been having a go, never having done it before. She's doing better. But then she's younger. Well, in my head she is younger. But actually, she isn't. Somehow my mind had frozen her at the age she was when we first met – a decade ago. Even though I know perfectly well that time passes in North Wales at exactly the rate it does in Cheshire.

I wonder whether something similar happens when we think about Mary. Not long ago, and not for the first time, we were imagining a young teenager being told that she was going to have a baby, and somehow – for me at least – Mary has remained a nervous young woman.

But 30 years have passed.

Mary has now produced other sons, something that earned women respect then, as now, in some communities. She is a widow[1] – Joseph disappears from the Gospel accounts after the family's visit to the temple when Jesus was 12. She is in her mid-forties. Far from nervous, John tells us she expects the servants at the wedding banquet to do as she says.

Hold *that* Mary in your mind's eye.

Then picture another scene. There's something you really want to do – go to a concert, or to a particular place, or meet a certain person. And somebody offers you the opportunity. You feel a mixture of nerves, excitement, a desire to delay maybe. What do you say? 'I couldn't possibly.' 'No, really, I couldn't.' It's something you really want to do, but the moment is overwhelming.

Now, bring together those two images to form an impression of what happens in this moment when the Gospel writer launches Jesus' ministry.

It's the third day of the banquet. In those days weddings lasted virtually a whole week, but even so by the third day, plenty had been eaten and drunk. This was different from running out of champagne just before the best man's speech. It might have curtailed the festivities, but the groom would still have already provided three days' worth of food and wine.

Mary sees the problem, and she knows Jesus can help. She has, after all, spent 30 years watching her son. She knew who Jesus was and she'd observed people were beginning to follow him. So when she sees that the steward has no more wine she lets Jesus know. 'They have no more wine.'

Jesus – and let's not forget he was fully human – feels that natural resistance come upon him that comes on us just before we move on to do something new. 'What concern is that to you and me – they'll be fine, they don't need me to interfere.' 'My hour hasn't come yet'. 'I couldn't possibly.' Jesus needed, as I have often needed, a final push from someone who has confidence in me.

Mary tells the stewards to do whatever Jesus tells them, then she rocks back on one heel a bit, looks at Jesus and with a look asks, 'Now what are you going to do?'

Wonder: one woman's story

If there is a day in the church calendar when I am most frequently disappointed by the sermon, it is Easter Day. Despite the fact that Easter Sunday's main service is often 'all age' in some way, I doubt very much that hollow chocolate eggs, eating daffodils, pushing cream pies in the preacher's face or any of the other gimmicks I've witnessed over the years, really convey the wonder of the resurrection.

The problem with these sermons, it seems to me, is that they are generic. They try to convey a proposition, or a belief, rather than sticking to the Bible passage set for the day. In an article I co-wrote with a colleague in *The Preacher* magazine (2019) we commented on the fact that we had both been told, of this most significant of days in the Christian calendar: 'Don't worry. You don't have to preach on the text at Easter.' And reviewing Easter sermons available online and on paper, it seems many don't. Ignoring the text, and opting for propositional preaching, largely results in generic sermons that fail to enter into the wonder of Easter. Inviting hearers into an encounter with the risen Jesus offers richer possibilities.

So, when I was invited to preach one Easter Sunday, I decided to focus on the reading set for the day, John 20.1–18, Mary of Magdala's story. I quoted the first part of this sermon in Chapter 1 – here it is in its entirety.

Sermon

'It is finished.' That's what Jesus had said just two days ago. 'It is finished.' His life was finished. His work was finished. His mission to the world, to break through human hardness, human pride, human insistence on religion that had little to do with God. 'It is finished.'

And it was. Finished. The expert executioners had already beaten him. They knew, from years of experience, when a person was dead. And this one was definitely finished.

And so, when Mary went to the tomb two days later she went without hope. She went to tend a dead friend. To do the very last thing she could do for the dead one she had followed.

He was gone. Perhaps she began to realize that although to Jesus she *was* someone, a person worth listening to, a person to walk with, that too was finished. She was once again the woman from whom demons had been cast out. The woman who down through history was to be remembered as of ill-repute rather than a woman of courageous faith.

The tomb was her focus. A place to remember. A place to grieve. A place of death.

But when she got to the tomb, it was a tomb no longer. The stone was rolled back. The body was gone. The tomb was broken open.

She ran to Peter and the nameless one, the one whom Jesus loved.

Her concern was for the tomb – not only had they taken Jesus' life, they had taken his body too. Now it really was all finished.

The disciples ran. They too were focused on the tomb.

The disciple Jesus loved got there first. He looked and saw strips of cloth lying there. Not quite an empty tomb, but nothing to entice him in.

Peter though, impetuous Peter, ran inside. Maybe for him it already was finished. He had misunderstood Jesus so many times. And at the last, when Jesus needed a friend, Peter had denied even knowing him. On this the first day of the week, he entered a place of death and became unclean himself. Touching death meant you couldn't come before God without making a sacrifice. But Peter went inside because, probably, he already felt a gulf between himself and God. His grief for Jesus was mixed with horror at himself, and something inside him had died too.

Finally, the other disciple stooped and entered the tomb. He saw the abandoned grave clothes. He believed.

We don't know what he believed, of course, and he hadn't understood. Perhaps, in the context of the times, he believed that Jesus had become a god, like some of the Roman emperors had after death. Perhaps he thought Jesus had been a god pretending to be human, as happened in some mythology.

But it was finished, so he and Peter returned home. Jesus was dead. The body was gone. Nothing more to be done.

But Mary ... Mary hangs around. Maybe she just wants to feel close to Jesus. Maybe there remains inside her some hidden, flickering flame of hope.

Somehow or other she wants to be close to her Lord. It's probably something we've all done, I know I have. You go to a particular place to remember someone special, or feel close to them somehow. For Mary the tomb is not the point. When the angels ask why she is crying it all comes out – she is looking for Jesus.

Whatever she may think, Mary knows she doesn't know. And it is in her not knowing that she sees. When the men looked into the tomb they saw evidence – no body, empty grave clothes. When Mary looks in she sees angels. When Mary looks into the tomb it is already sanctified.

While she is looking into a sanctified grave, someone approaches her – someone who is wandering the garden. He asks the same question, 'Why are you crying?' He goes a step further, 'Who are you looking for?' And Mary gives more or less the same answer – she is looking for Jesus.

And then he says her name.

From the very depths of darkness, the little light of hope begins to burn brighter, and then bursts into radiant flame. Jesus says her name. He knows her. He is here, in this moment, for her. The one she mourns, the dead one, is fully, completely, vibrantly alive. Joy and delight thrill through her veins. Her mind is on fire. Her heart burns. The world is wonderfully, completely, radiantly changed. It will never, it can never, be the same again. Life has burst out of the grave. Life in all its fullness has filled the world. In the uttering of one word, her name, Jesus has told Mary all that she needs to know in order to worship.

Life has invaded the tomb. Remembering is about resurrection not death. Grief is infused with joy. Death is defeated.

Mary wants to hold on to Jesus, make him hers, this Lord once dead and now alive.

But Jesus cannot be held. He is not hers, he is not ours. It is not her task, nor ours, to pin Jesus down, to define him, to explain him, to understand him. It is her task, and ours, to release him into the world, to go and to tell. And why would we not? This is not an idea that can be explained, a doctrine to be taught. This is a new world, a new way of living, a new era in which life not death is the natural order.

On that morning, many years ago, the tomb was open and death was broken. Re-creation burst out like water from a geyser, like a new baby being pushed into the world. And nothing could hold him. And now we live in a world where the life revolution has begun, God's vitality is filling this place and all places, love is pushing out hate and light is shining out. Darkness and death cannot beat it, change it, hide it, kill it, stop it. It is finished.

Easter Day is the day that shocked the world. It still does.

Easter Day is the day when the world was invaded with resurrection life. It still is.

We see one final thing in Mary. Life's invasion of death, God's invasion of the world, happens through Jesus' followers. The invasion is to go on through Jesus' disciples. Even in the joy of meeting her risen Lord Mary had a task – 'go and tell'.

It is a task we share. We, also, are to go and tell.

Valuing women

Locating Bible women in the narrative of God's people reveals that, though small in number, they occupy a whole range of roles, more similar to men than different from them. Lindsay Hardin Freeman (2014: 461) points out that while 'women were not known as warriors or judges' Deborah was both; 'women were not known as killers', yet Jael and Judith dispatched key enemy leaders; while women were not priests, when Hannah, Hagar and Rebekah cried out in prayer, God heard; women were not known for negotiating, but two unnamed women – the woman of Tekoa,[2] and the woman of Abel[3] – were among the best; while women are not named as disciples, some of Jesus' closest and most faithful allies were women. When Saul needed advice he sought the witch of Endor; when Mary and Joseph took their baby to the temple Anna recognized him. Some of the best biblical poetry comes from women: Miriam, Deborah, Hannah and Mary.

Women in the Gospels are often misread, particularly when preconceptions override what is actually on the page. One of the women who suffers from this is the woman who anoints Jesus' feet at the house of Simon the Pharisee in Luke 7. This is from a sermon I gave just before the General Election of 2015:

Sermon snippet

It seems not to matter which paper you read, in 11 days' time the nation will divide into two camps, based on our attitude to the other. Are other people useful to us, worthy of our attention, somebody else's ex-pats or our immigrants?

I don't want to comment on how to vote – if you would like to think about a Christian perspective present and past, archbishops have given very thoughtful responses.

It seems to me that the story we had read invites us to consider the question, however. How we see things is important. How

---

the people in the story see things gives us some clues about Jesus' seeing.

Simon is a religious leader, a significant figure in the town. He's invited Jesus to dinner not so much as an honour but as a means of entertainment. He places Jesus opposite him so that the whole table can hear their discussion, and presumably enjoy Simon's takedown of this itinerant preacher.

He does not offer Jesus the culturally standard hospitality, no appropriate greeting. He does not kiss Jesus in welcome, nor wash the dust of the road from his feet. Simon has already decided that Jesus is insignificant, and treats him that way.

As a human being Jesus clearly felt the snub.

Human beings use a snub to put others in their place, don't they? It's so much more civilized than saying what you really think.

A couple of weeks ago I was invited to teach some church leaders in training. I'd been asked to talk about women in leadership. When I arrived the students wanted to follow this theme by looking at key Bible passages, and so that's what we did for a couple of hours. Towards the end of the session one of the guys said to me, 'Did you say you're married? Because that's really cool. Not many women who think like you can get a husband, can they?'

For a moment I felt like a freak. I had been snubbed.

That man hadn't heard a word I said. He didn't really see me.

Luke tells us that there was a woman in this house. We know she was there before Jesus arrived, because he says she had kissed him since he came in. Her estimation of Jesus is entirely different – she worships him.

The tradition surrounding this story presents the woman as a prostitute, who realizes how bad she is – Luke, after all, has her as a 'sinner in the town' – falls at Jesus' feet and is forgiven by him. But how can that make sense?

Why does she worship someone she hasn't met before? How does she know that he is God, and simultaneously just happen to have a jar of expensive ointment on hand if they have never met? And most importantly, if it is her expensive gift, or her expansive worship that earn her salvation, where is the need for grace?

That version of the story doesn't work. The woman is already in the house when Jesus arrives – perhaps she is a daughter, or a slave of the household. She knows who Jesus is. Perhaps she has met him before.

Aha! You might say, but we know she is a sinner. That's true. But elsewhere in Luke (5.8) we read that Peter is a sinner. No one has ever suggested that Peter was a prostitute, though. And anyway, think about the relative positions of the people involved. At the table, Jesus, as well as everyone else, would have sat with their feet *behind* them. To wash someone's feet required you to *be* behind them. To ply the trade of a prostitute, however, a woman needed to be *in front* of potential clients. The story as traditionally told simply doesn't work.

It seems to me that this woman belonged to the household, had met Jesus previously and been forgiven, and was now in a place of worship.

Simon, of course, is incensed. How can a woman deflect attention from him? As he fumes inwardly, Jesus turns to him.

'Simon, do you see this woman?'

'Do you *see* this woman?'

Another sermon in which I explored the potential power of women, rather than allow them to be trivialized, was on the 'wise' and 'foolish' bridesmaids (Matthew 25). Looked at from a feminist perspective, it seemed to me that the bridegroom rather than the bridesmaids were to blame for their predicament, and that, actually, there was enough oil anyway.

Sermon snippet

For most of my life, I think I have wanted to be one of the wise bridesmaids. They seem to get all the accolades. They were ready. They had enough oil. The bridegroom welcomes them in; the bridegroom – Jesus – it's been assumed. He comes again and the wise are ready – full of good deeds and constant faith.

The foolish ones simply weren't ready. They didn't meet the deadline. They hadn't used their time wisely. They weren't motivated. Poor foolish bridesmaids!

It all seems so simple. The wise, ready. The foolish, unprepared. Well, let's look again.

What exactly is the difference between the wise and the foolish? They had all accepted the invitation to the wedding. They had all assembled waiting for the bridegroom to come. They had all fallen asleep when he takes longer than expected.

And then five have enough oil and five run out and have to get more.

But – isn't there actually enough oil for everyone? Couldn't they have shared lamps? Shouldn't the bridegroom have arrived on time? And shouldn't he have come with a bride?

Jesus tells this parable not to people like the blind man he recently healed. Not to people like the children he told his disciples to welcome. Not even to those like the palm-waving crowds who welcomed him to Jerusalem. He tells this story to people who think they are wise, like the bridesmaids. He tells it to the religious leaders; those who think they have stored up plenty of good deeds, who expect to be in power when the Messiah comes. They have been waiting for a long time for this delayed bridegroom Messiah. And as they waited, they have made it increasingly impossible for ordinary people to be ready. They've increased the costs of sacrifices, so the poor ran out. They constantly imposed new rules, so people couldn't be prepared.

And what kind of a bridegroom is it who arrives at the wedding feast alone? He has entered a covenant. His partner should be there too.

What is happening in this story?

We have someone in control of the others and their resources. There is enough oil, but its value increases because demand for it is artificially increased. Those who have are able to exploit and eventually eliminate those who have not.

The bridegroom is not God. The wise bridesmaids show self-interest. The foolish bridesmaids have no power to increase their resources.

It is not a story of how things should be, but of how they are.

It is telling that this is the first of three parables in which Jesus talks about the commonwealth of God. And immediately after them people plot to kill him.

Make women count

A quick review of Old Testament passages included in the Common Worship Lectionary for reading on Sundays, the passages most church people are likely to encounter, therefore, reveals how the Bible has been rendered *his*-story. For the purposes of this chapter, I reread the passages included between February 2013 and February 2019. Women are almost always presented as problematic, or an adjunct of men. We have the story of Isaac meeting Rebekah, Jacob being tricked into marrying both Leah and Rachel, and Sarah's ill-treatment of Hagar. Shiphrah and Puah are present, within a longer story. Hannah appears only as staying at home until Samuel is weaned, and then offering him for service in the temple. Bathsheba appears as the woman with whom David commits adultery, otherwise everything about David is good news. From 1 Kings, Jezebel makes an appearance as an evil woman, and later (2 Kings) Naaman's slave girl stands out as a godly one.

If Thomas Carlyle was right in saying 'The history of the world is but the biography of great men', then it is equally true that the story of the Old Testament has become little more than the story of certain men. Here's a snippet from a sermon that tries to restore Sarah to her rightful place:

Sermon snippet

'Come for a barbecue, we'll have burgers and yoghurt.' The wife makes the bread. The servants kill and cook the calf. Abraham sets before his guests the food that *he* has prepared.

It's a familiar story.

Possibly Abraham recognized these visitors as messengers of God, but he does no more than show the hospitality typical of the Middle East even today.

Then it gets awkward. 'Where's your wife?' Specifically, 'Where is your wife Sarah?'

Abraham's history is a bit chequered. His wife, apparently, is

---

also his sister. He has treated her variously as a possession and as a pawn. When God called Abram he took Sarai with him – there is no evidence he spoke to her about their forthcoming journey. When they end up going to Egypt because of famine in the land, Abram says, 'Say you are my sister so it will go well with *me.*' There is no concern about how it will go with her.

Abraham already knows that she is integral to God's plan, it is she who will be the bearer of God's promise, but apparently Abraham hasn't told her. She remains expendable.

Perhaps, when the guests ask Abraham where Sarah is, he has the grace to blush and look down at his sandals in embarrassment. Maybe.

Sarah, I think, knows that Abraham is to be God's covenant bearer. That's why she gave him her slave some time ago. But she doesn't know that she too is part of the plan. When one of the guests suggests that she is to have a child, she laughs. Even now she isn't part of a conversation that concerns her so intimately.

Sarah must have got used to overhearing things about herself over the years. Perhaps there was gossip when Abraham married his sister, or perhaps others envied her his wealth. As time went by there might have been subtle, and not so subtle, hints about the patter of tiny feet. As her barrenness became more apparent maybe there was pity, for her or for Abraham. Finally, when it was obviously too late, it could be there was gossip about whose sin had prevented the continuation of Abraham's line through her. And at last, as age advanced, it's conceivable that people stopped talking about her, and Sarah retreated, relieved, into the shadows.

And now, she is being talked about again. And it's about children again. And if it happens it will be so remarkable that she will be the topic of gossip – again! I'm not sure how she laughs, but I bet there is more than a hint of irony in it.

Sarah hasn't really counted for anything since she married. She's been taken – by Abraham to a different country, by Pharaoh's talent scouts to Pharaoh, because she is attractive. She's been asked to lie for her husband. She's been judged as barren. She's been mocked by her servant girl.

But to God, she is just as much the bearer of a covenant as is her husband.

'Women in the Bible do not shuffle onto its pages; they stride across, with their heads held high and their hearts full of passion' (Freeman, 2014: 391). One such is Abigail. A beautiful woman, as seems often required in Old Testament stories, she is also a woman of understanding (1 Sam. 25.3). Her husband, on the other hand, is 'surly and mean'. I have never heard a sermon about Abigail. Perhaps part of the reason is that even the NRSVA entitles the story 'David and the wife of Nabal'!

Sermon snippet

In previous sermons we've spent time with David, the man after God's own heart. He's been described as 'humble', 'reverent', 'respectful', 'trusting', 'loving', 'devoted', 'faithful' and 'obedient'. He has come out of our sermon series very well, has David. Of course, he has the advantage of self-reporting, because all our texts so far have come from psalms David wrote.

So, this week, I want to look at David in a different light. Through a story that someone else tells, about something David actually does – or nearly does.

In this story, David is on the run with his outlaws. They are holed up in an area dominated by a wealthy landowner. It seems that they did the rich man's shepherds no harm, and may even have protected them from others. So when David decides to have a feast, he asks the wealthy man to recognize what he has done for him and donate some food. The rich man sends David's messengers away with a flea in their ear, and David, incensed, decides to go and kill him. It's one proud man standing against another proud man in a fight to show who is most powerful.

Seeing the ridiculousness of the situation, the rich man's wife, Abigail, prepares food on his behalf and takes it to David. This is not submission or surrender though. Even as she offers the food to David, Abigail makes clear what David was about to do: shed blood by his own hand, without just cause. The man we have come to know as 'a man after God's own heart' was angered because someone refused him food. His solution was destruction. Abigail has the wisdom to see what needs to be done, and the

> courage to do it. David is preserved from the consequences of his
> own foolish pride by the wisdom of a woman.

Finding a role model

Much of the way we understand the Bible relies on imagination. We interpret it through the lens of our own experience;
or retell it imaginatively, using metaphor or imagery; or think
ourselves into its various scenes. Many familiar stories have
been altered over time as imagination has been impacted by
cultural or historical changes. Take, for example, the treatment
of Martha of Bethany in the first six centuries of the Christian
Church.

In a 2018 TV production, biblical historians Joan Taylor and
Helen Bond traced the story of some of Jesus' women disciples.
A striking feature of their investigation was looking at images
carved on stone coffins held in the Vatican museum, Rome.
The sarcophagi all depict the story of Jesus on his way to Bethany, where Lazarus has died. The earliest image (from the third
century) depicts Jesus with Lazarus in the tomb, Mary kneeling
by Jesus and Martha behind him. The women are bareheaded
and the same size as the men. By the fourth century, Martha
has disappeared and Mary is veiled and bowing in subservient fashion. In a later image, Mary has bowed so low and
become so small that she appears as a kind of footstool. The
artwork illustrates what has happened not only visually but
also through the many retellings of the story.

My point is that imagination always plays a role in Bible
reading. What follows is part of a talk I gave at Women's
Voices 2017, based on what we know and what I conjecture
about a woman Paul met during his travels recorded in the
book of Acts.

She is a good woman.
She works with her hands.
She trades in fabrics, she provides food for her household
and tasks for her servant girls.
She buys and sells and makes a profit.
She opens her home to others and shows hospitality.
She makes cloth of fine purple.
She looks to the ways of her household.

If you are familiar with Proverbs 31, you might think I am about to speak of the woman who apparently is the answer to that question, 'Who can find a good wife?' Except I did say earlier that all three of my women are from the New Testament. The woman I want us to think about is Lydia. We find her in Acts 16, and her story made it into the Lectionary this year! The Lectionary is the pattern of readings set for Church of England churches through-out the year. On the Sixth Sunday after Easter this year Lydia's story was included. Unfortunately, it was paired with a reading from John's Gospel where Jesus promises the Holy Spirit to those who love him, and with Ezekiel's vision of dry bones coming to life.

I'm going to guess that in most churches Lydia didn't get a look in.

I find Lydia intriguing. Some commentators say Luke invented her to make a point, and she didn't exist at all. Others say she did. Some say she was highly regarded; others say she wasn't. Some say she was rich, others say she wasn't.

You get the picture.

I want to talk about Lydia in the context in which Luke and Paul meet her. Luke is travelling with Paul at this stage, and they arrive in the town of Philippi. The Lydia they meet has a geographic, political, economic and religious context and I hope we might learn something from them.

Philippi was a thoroughly Roman city, founded by Mark Anthony in 42 BCE on the site of an older Macedonian settlement. Roman gods were worshipped, Latin was spoken. It was a garrison town, full of soldiers. Men dominated. While on active service Roman soldiers were forbidden to marry, and so in their garrison towns they would 'buy' women for sexual and other purposes. It was regarded as normal that in order for men to function properly in the work they had to do, they needed access to women they could use however they saw fit. Not unlike the *Daily Mail*'s justification for photographing the legs of a human rights lawyer rather than spend time writing about her achievements.

Philippi might not have been fertile ground for the gospel – love, service and equality are rarely regarded as great virtues in testosterone-fuelled cultures.

The city *was*, however, a great place to deal in symbols of power and privilege. And that meant purple.

Let me tell you a bit about purple. Purple was special. Only the high-born and powerful in Roman society were allowed to wear it. It was an expensive symbol of consequence and prestige. And Tyrian purple was the best.

Lydia dealt in very high-quality goods.

Purple was derived from the mucus of the hypobrachial gland of the murex brandaris – sea snails. Apparently, it took thousands of them to get a gram of dye, and animal urine was integral to the process. For obvious reasons the process took place outside the city limits. Those involved in it were likely to have smelled too. They probably didn't get out much. Just because they made a costly product did not mean the workers were respected. The global textile industry of today is little different in terms of the way workers are treated.

Plutarch, the Greek philosopher, wrote that: 'Often we take pleasure in a thing, but we despise the one who made it. Thus we value ... purple clothing, but the dyers ... remain for us common and low.'

The elite classes tend to despise and resent manufacturers and dealers even now. Wearers of Saville Row suits must live with the fact that somewhere there is a tailor who knows their measurements.

Lydia may well have been wealthy and influential. She was also a householder. Economically Lydia might have been doing well, but socially she probably wasn't invited to the best parties.

Maybe she found comfort in religion. She was sympathetic to the Jewish faith, a God-fearer. Well, working with cloth wasn't great from that perspective either. In 2 Samuel 3 when David was having a rant and cursing the house of Joab, he says this:

> May the house of Joab never be without one who has a discharge, or who is leprous, or who holds a spindle,[4] or who falls by the sword, or who lacks food.

Right in the middle of as many awful things he could wish on an enemy as he can think of – sickness and swords and starvation – comes working in textiles, or perhaps doing woman's work. May they never be without some grim deaths, some awful illnesses and someone who works with cloth.

So who might Lydia have been? I think she was a woman of influence, an astute dealer in exclusive merchandise and well known in the town. At the same time, I think she was marginalized socially and by her religion. Therefore, when she went to pray, she went outside the town to the river.

Paul and Luke could not have expected to find a synagogue in Philippi. So, when Sabbath came they went outside the city to the river looking for a place of prayer.

It's an interesting, though time-consuming, exercise to look through commentaries on this passage. It tells you more about the commentator than it does about Paul or Luke, it seems to me. Some want to insist that this would be a semi-Christian, God-fearing gathering; others accept that people gathered by rivers to worship whatever god they thought they knew, and Paul and Luke went in search of anyone who was looking for a god. In Athens, Paul wasn't that bothered about a semi-Christian god, he just declared the unknown god, starting from where the Athenians were, so I imagine he took the same approach in Philippi. Riverbanks were used to gather and pray when there was no place of worship within the city. Down by the river outside Philippi, Paul and Luke come across Lydia with a group of women she leads, her household, who are praying to God. They talk to the women and Lydia becomes their first convert on European soil. She and her household were baptized.

Now for a bit of speculation. Philippi was full of men who were away from home. Their 'need' of prostitutes was acknowledged and catered for. In communities like this, women get ill in ways that make them no longer saleable. This left them with no way of making a living. Extracting snot from sea snails to make dye with animal urine was the kind of unpleasant job that ex-sex workers might turn to. Lydia was a God-fearing woman. She knew that God expected God's people to show charity. How might Lydia have come to have a household of women? It is perfectly possible, I think, that not only was the first church on European soil made up of women, run by a woman, working in a trade despised in the Hebrew Bible, many of these women might also have been rescued or removed from the sex trade. Wouldn't that make an inconvenient story?

Lydia is most definitely not the 'good wife' of Proverbs 31. The woman in Proverbs does manufacture cloth, but in the home and for her family. Her spinning is interwoven with other domestic duties. She provides for her husband, and it is he who is respected within the city. It is he who becomes the leader because of her endeavour. Not so Lydia.

Lydia is a leader in business and in the church. She isn't mentioned in Paul's letter to the church in Philippi, though. What does that mean? One commentator suggested that her involvement in the business world hindered her work in the church. I think there are other more adequate explanations. Perhaps Lydia was so obviously a leader she didn't need to be mentioned. Or perhaps she was a leader at work or in the city, and did not spend a great deal of time leading the church. It's too easy to look for significance within the structure of the church, and it makes us miss what God and people are doing elsewhere.

Lydia protected her household, she provided work for others, she had a voice in the city. She transformed the lowly into the beautiful, both in terms of her cloth and possibly her workers. Perhaps Lydia's home is recognized by Paul as a model of inclusion – where there is no Jew or Gentile, slave or free, male or female for those who are one in Christ.

Building communality

I've suggested previously that 'communality' is both a biblical principle and something that required commitment to unity above agreement. Relationship, it seems, is key to women's development in faith, and so it is perhaps among biblical women where examples of communality can be found.

We looked briefly in the Introduction at Queen Vashti, how she set an example for others and paved the way for Esther. The next sermon explores communality in the story of Mary and Martha. It was specifically written for a group about to embark on a period of community living.

Sermon

First of all, by God, BELIEVE IN SOMETHING.

The final words of my last sermon when I spoke to the wider community of ordinands.

Believe in something.

Part way through the story we just heard read, Jesus prompts Martha to say what it is she believes in. And somehow Martha arrives at a statement that makes her the first person to really understand who Jesus is. She moves all the way from, 'If you'd come when I asked this wouldn't have happened', to 'You are the Christ, the Son of God, *who is coming*.' From scepticism – 'If you had only come' – to belief – 'You *are* the coming one.' Not simply you have yet to come, but you have come, you do come and you will come.

It seems that throughout the Church's history, Martha has been the 'busy one', the one who couldn't stop and listen to Jesus. She has a bad reputation in some ways. There isn't much you can do with Martha's story. She didn't set an example of quiet listening; she didn't use expensive perfume to anoint Jesus' feet. Martha, it sometimes seems, was the solid, boring type; dependable, but unexciting.

Yet John suggests otherwise. Jesus loved Martha – and her sister. Jesus loved *Martha*. It's easy to look around at other people

---

and see why they might have been selected for ordination, why God might call them, but (for me at least) I really struggled to see why God, or the Church, might want me to be ordained. I can see good things in other people, but I struggle to see the same things in myself.

It's Martha who realizes who Jesus is. And she does it because she is engaged with what is going on around her. She hasn't separated herself from the crowd, she is part of it. It's only when she goes to meet Jesus on the road that she appears to be alone with him and he calls out of her a believing she didn't know she had.

There are some things we just know, I think. Without evidence, without rational thought, without demonstration – we just know some things to be true. I understand from a Jewish friend that there is a Hebrew word for this kind of knowing. It means something like 'you know in your knower' – whatever part of us it is. It's how we know some things. It's a different kind of knowing from being aware that 2+2 usually make 4, or that a deadline is on the horizon, or that a friend needs us to have coffee with them, or that summer is coming. It's a more centred knowing, a knowing that forms us into who we are. It happens when we believe in something or, more accurately, someone.

I can almost picture Martha getting to the end of her sentence and stopping, surprised: 'Did I really say that? Where did that come from?' She had brought to her consciousness a knowing that had already formed.

That he is the Christ who *comes*.

And then we learn something else.

'When Martha had said this she went and called her sister Mary, privately. The Teacher is calling for you.'

Maybe you feel a bit like Mary.

A bad thing has happened. Her friend has let her down. She doesn't go out to meet him. Perhaps she's resentful? Or sulking? Or just unsure?

Whatever Mary feels, she seems to be in a dark place. Her brother has died; Jesus did not come when asked; her friends are gathered around her to comfort her. She is walking in the dark.

In her book *Learning to Walk in the Dark* (2014), Barbara Brown Taylor writes:

I have learned things in the dark that I could never have learned in the light, things that have saved my life over and over again, so that there is really only one logical conclusion. I need darkness as much as I need light. (82)

We do need dark times, but we also need friends like Martha to call us out of the dark times; to make us aware that Jesus comes to *us*.

Once Martha has realized that Jesus is the Christ, the Son of God who *comes*, she goes to her sister and tells her, 'Jesus has come for you too.' And Mary believes enough to respond and go to meet Jesus on the road.

It's no accident that they meet on the road: Martha who has voiced her more developed belief; Mary who has responded to Martha's invitation, 'He's come for you too'; and Jesus. Jesus and his disciples don't make it to the village, Mary and Martha end up going where they hadn't intended to go – they all end up somewhere different, because they are together.

There's one more member of this small community as it travels together that I want to mention.

If A. A. Milne had written about Jesus' disciples Thomas would have been Eeyore, wouldn't he? At the start of the story Jesus is in a different community. He's with his disciples. They're feeling a bit vulnerable, because not long ago some people tried to kill Jesus. So when the message comes that Lazarus is ill and Jesus tells them he's just sleeping, they're inclined to leave well alone. 'If things are fine, let's not get involved.' Then it gets a bit embarrassing because Jesus says, 'Actually Lazarus is dead', and there's a conflict in each of them – following Jesus, yes, but not wanting to be so committed that things get awkward. Nervousness and a desire to keep things stable, mixed with *knowing* that they should go.

Finally, Thomas, that great motivational speaker, pipes up, 'Let's go with him so that we may die.'

What might we have said? 'Come on, it'll probably end in tears, but a deal's a deal and we said we'd follow him.' Neither Thomas nor the other disciples seem to want to be where they are going. They are reluctant, resentful even. But because Thomas manages to be resentfully obedient they go. And what do they see? The first resurrection!

For Thomas and the others Jesus had already come, in some ways. But they needed to understand that Jesus is not only the Christ who has come, but also the Christ who *comes*. The anxiety of the world beginning to turn against Jesus raised questions for them, but as they followed, however reluctantly, they saw new things.

Today we come together as part of the wider community to form a unique community. A community of people coming to the end of their studies; a community of people here both to learn and to meditate and to remember the events of Easter in a way that we never have before and never will do again; a community of people soon to be ordained into ministry in the Church of England.

Our personalities, our faith, our stories will affect how we contribute to the formation of that community, just as the characters within the story we just read affect what happens in it.

I don't believe that this is just Easter School.

I don't believe that this is just a course requirement.

I don't believe that this is an imposition on time we should be spending at home.

I don't believe that this is the precursor to the blessed relief of some time off.

I believe that each of us is called to this community.

I believe that each of us is called to be part of this community.

I believe that there is potential in this community for each of us to gain a deeper knowledge of Jesus: to call others into that same place to journey with others and with Jesus to a place we might otherwise not have gone.

But I also believe this. In order for any of us to help build this community so that we can fulfil our potential as disciples, and leave with a renewed and deepened faith, we have, like Martha, Mary and even Thomas, to believe something just enough to make us act on it. We need individually to be committed to the best of what this week might bring.

There is no pressure. Just a question: what – for God's sake and for the sake of others – do you believe you are called to this week?

Time for reflection

We come now to reflect on the task of preaching for women.

1. *Affirming women*
   Look back over some previous sermons. *Did you find a woman in the margins of the story? Did you affirm women in your sermon?*

   Look at your next sermon text. *Is there something in it for women? Does it reveal something about women?*

2. A prayer and a promise. *Could you make these words a commitment for your preaching?*

   Take me as I am
   A woman – sometimes silenced, sometimes oppressed.
   Take me as a preacher, with a voice to speak your words.
   Make me brave.
   Make me honest.
   Send me to seek the silenced.
   Send me to hear the demeaned.
   Call out your image through my story.
   Complete your image through me.

Notes

1 While Joseph is mentioned by Luke in 2.48, the story of the 12-year-old Jesus remaining behind at the temple, he drops out of the later story.
2 2 Samuel 14.
3 2 Samuel 20.
4 'Spindle' is one possible interpretation, preferred in some versions.

7

Preaching as a Woman

I set out in this book to explore reasons why women preachers might preach as women. We reflected on the kind of world we live in, and how a patriarchal narrative affects women's lives and experience. I want to move on now to thinking about how women preachers can fulfil the commission to speak to *this* congregation on *this* day from *this* text.

My vision is that of preacher as host, and preaching as 'the art of engaging the people of God in their shared narrative by creatively and hospitably inviting them into an exploration of biblical text, by means of which, corporately and individually, they might encounter the divine'. For those of us who want to speak intentionally as women, from women's bodies and women's experiences, there is an additional aim: to engage those of God's people who might find themselves on the margins of sermons.

In this chapter I want to suggest a model of preaching that enables us to explore biblical text from often silenced perspectives. It opens new spaces for women listeners, with the potential that they might meet God in new ways. It will be helpful if we begin with a sermon, so that I can show how the model worked in this particular instance. In this sermon, insight into the story was prompted by experience, although the story itself is about a man.

Sermon snippet

Where did he belong, this man with the trappings of wealth and education and lifestyle?

He knew sure enough who he belonged *to*. His employer.

She called the shots. Told him what to do, when and where. She controlled his life.

True, he enjoyed all the finer things – luxury, fine food, the best company, opulent travel.

But he was not free.

That was the cost.

He had been chosen for his skill, his integrity, his ability – chosen for a life of sumptuousness. But in return, he belonged. He was a possession, a valuable resource. All hope of a future had been removed from him. He would not be the head of a family, the father of generations. All hope of a future had been taken away, and he had no chance of resisting.

He knew who he belonged *to* all right.

But who did he belong *with*?

Not the friends of his youth. He was different now. No longer one of them.

Not with other worshippers of God, either. He was only allowed to participate in worship just so far. No approaching the sanctuary for him.

Where *did* he belong? Who *was* like him?

As he read, he thought he saw a glimpse of such a one. Someone like him. Someone who had been taken, and seized and wounded without protest. Someone humiliated. Someone to whom justice had also been denied. A man with no future, just like him.

Could he belong somehow?

A tiny flicker of hope sparked within him. Maybe he wasn't alone.

And then he realized, he wasn't alone, someone was alongside him. Someone attentive to him. Someone ready to listen.

With nothing to lose he asked, 'Who is this person who seems like me?'

And Philip explains where the eunuch belongs. He belongs in the family of God, as a follower of Jesus.

The good news resonates with this man who has had his future and his name taken from him. 'What's to stop me being baptized?' he asks. He may well have expected Philip to list off some reasons – he was, according to the law, defective and unclean. But Philip can see no objection, and the man is baptized. I wonder whether, at that point, he felt restored. Perhaps he was given a name again. Perhaps his baptism was a sign that he did now have a place to belong.

And Philip is moved on, to more people who do not know where they belong.

The world is full of Ethiopian eunuchs.

People who don't belong. Whose lives are controlled by others. Who seem to have everything and yet yearn for something different.

Recently we have heard about the Windrush scandal. People who thought they belonged, yet were told to go. And then the minister responsible for the guilty department also being told she no longer belonged, and should go.

My sister runs a charity for people who cannot access community fully because they are full-time carers for others. They are different, and so become forgotten.

My husband and I support Christians Against Poverty and are mindful of the extent to which employers control the lives of so many people without having to pay them, unless absolutely necessary, through zero-hours contracts.

Our local park is cleaned and tidied each morning by a group of people who have learning difficulties. They do a valuable job, yet I notice very few wishing them 'good morning'.

The world is full of Ethiopian eunuchs. Maybe, today, you are one of these marginalized people.

But God also sends Philips.

People who will walk alongside. People who will listen. Eventually perhaps people who will share the good news of Jesus.

Maybe this week you are called to walk with someone who feels marginalized, or alone. Maybe you are called to share faith with someone who is wondering whether they might belong.

God came in human form, and God still does.

Society creates Ethiopian eunuchs – people who are poor can be portrayed as lazy, when in fact they are working two or sometimes even three jobs to keep as much food as they can on the table. Disputes about important things can become two-sided battles in which some are painted as vindictive and mean-spirited. From the outside that appears to have been what happened in the tragic case of Alfie Evans.[1]

The church creates its own Ethiopian eunuchs of course. I don't think I am alone in being suspicious of those who seem to deride faith, or have no respect for the story of Jesus, or whatever it might be. It's easy to assign to the margins those people who come into church but don't know how to behave. Or to blame my inability to share my faith clearly on the world around, rather than on my own reluctance. Until recently I was happy enough to label members of the Humanist Society as wrong, or anti-Christian, or selfish or whatever. Now I know someone who goes to the Humanist Society, and I realize how wrong I have been.

Drawing alongside, listening, are important ways of developing relationships instead of increasing divides.

A hospitable model of preaching

In Chapter 1 I introduced a simple method of preparing to preach. It has six steps, beginning with Experience and Position, moving on to Tradition and Culture, and finally to Insight and Communication. The method is a route through the model of preaching below.

The method starts in one particular place, Experience. Other potential starting points, based on a four-source model of theological reflection, are Position, Culture and Tradition. It starts in the outer circle, and moves from there towards the sermon. I present the model in concentric circles to illustrate the cyclical process, and to highlight the fact that a sermon should always be the product of living a reflective life.

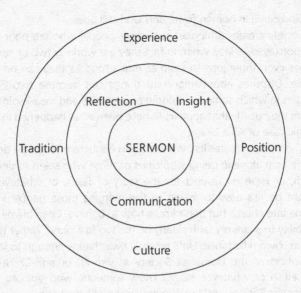

Starting with experience

Preaching as a woman fruitfully begins from Experience. I have argued that women's experience is distinctive and a useful entry into biblical text. Jesus frequently began encounters by asking about experience: according to Mark, Jesus took time to hear the whole story of the woman healed from bleeding; he knew the whole story of the woman who washed his feet with her hair; he listened to Martha's concerns on the way to the tomb of her brother; his heart went out to the widow of Nain. Homileticians have suggested a similar starting point. We have already heard from Tom Long (1988) that before saying something a preacher must see it, and from Fred Craddock (1979) that the sermon cannot be separated from the one delivering it. Before a preacher *says* something, a preacher must *see* something. To be a preacher is to be called to be a *witness,* one who sees before speaking, one whose right to speak has been created by what has been seen. Women writers have stressed a similar message, encouraging us to value truths forged from our own experience (Durber, 2007), and to 'announce to the ecclesial public [our] own narrative springing from the truth of [our] own story' (Copeland, 2014: 130).

In the sermon above, the experience of being marginalized led me to read the story from the perspective of the eunuch. Most often when I have heard the passage preached it has been from Philip's perspective, with injunctions that the congregation should copy him.

Step one

Experience and Position

Starting from Experience as we come to the Bible leads on to thinking about Position. I imagined the eunuch to be marginalized simply from hints in the text: he was alone; he was reading something he didn't understand; he had gone to Jerusalem to worship, despite the fact he was an ethnic minority and excluded from temple worship (Deut. 23.1–3; Lev. 21.18–20); he was going away from Jerusalem. Central to his experience, I identified loneliness, and the fact that he belonged to someone rather than with anyone. My Position was that people yearn for community, and behaviours and attitudes can lead to exclusion.

I need to say something about my Position with regard to preaching here, because what I am suggesting is time-consuming. I accept that there may be reasons why what we say on Sunday can only be prepared on Saturday, but I do not believe that sermons can be prepared in such a short space of time. It is perfectly possible to think of something to say. It is equally possible that God, by God's grace, will bless it. It is not, however, preaching. Preaching takes time. It derives from people, not from propositions. It relies on experience as much as education. It is also, when we commit to it, the most effective way of giving pastoral care, discipleship training and Christian education. During the rest of the week, no matter how many individual visits we make, or small groups we attend, we can never speak to as many people as we can on a Sunday morning when we preach to the wider congregation.

Tradition and Culture

Thinking about difference in a story about a eunuch led to research – how might Tradition inform the story? Step 3 in the method might include 'commentary work'. Commentaries, I believe, should be viewed with a healthy amount of scepticism. Although the situation is improving, most commentaries are written by white, academic men from the West, and overlook issues of inclusion and exclusion.[2]

Step two

Emerging themes

Pulling together themes that emerge from the four sources leads to a number of emerging themes. These, importantly, offer the opportunity of raising theological questions, including thinking about our own theology (Position).

Step three

Research

Research about eunuchs offered a range of interpretations. Theoretically, in the Roman Empire, castration was illegal. Eunuchs, however, were popular as guardians of the bedchamber, and could be purchased outside the Empire. Some gifted young men were castrated in order to fulfil particular functions, as might have been the case with this keeper of the queen's treasury. If something cannot be proved from the text but remains possible, I have no problem using it. Imaging the Ethiopian eunuch as having been made a eunuch in this way enabled me to identify parallels between his own story and the story he was reading.

Step four

Reflection and Insight

The previous steps have already begun to focus the sermon. Now comes the stage at which ideas and themes for preaching are narrowed down, and we begin to think about what we might actually say. Once we have an overall, rough idea, we need simply to 'live with it'. In some ways this is the equivalent of an athlete imagining themselves winning. I have found that if I cannot imagine myself comfortably saying what I think I have prepared, it is highly likely I should not be saying it. Dwelling with the prepared word means trusting our subconscious, but more importantly, I believe this is where the Spirit most often speaks directly, shaping and sculpting the work I have already done.

Step five

Communication

Having filtered the insights I might want to develop, the work of communication begins. Who am I speaking to, and how will this resonate with them? I mentioned some national events and issues in my sermon, but I also included one that was very local to the congregation. This is the step where I particularly weed out non-inclusive language. Communication includes not only the words I will use, and the way I use them. It also involves thinking about resonance – how the congregation might hear what I say – and subconscious communication – what I might say without intending to, or what I might say but not explicitly. In this example, I implied how the eunuch became a eunuch without saying so: 'All hope of a future had been removed from him.'

Step six

Final check

I was preaching on the morning of 31 August 1997. Fortunately I listened to the news. Some of my congregation arrived at church not knowing that Diana, Princess of Wales, had died. It served as a lesson in the importance of being as up-to-date as possible, before mounting the pulpit steps. I rapidly rewrote some of my sermon.

By contrast, I attended church on Sunday 16 September 2011. Nobody mentioned the events of the previous Tuesday. The worship songs were merry and bright, the sermon simple and trite. While there was to be a discussion that evening on the events of 9/11, its horror was not allowed to darken morning worship. To me, it jarred. If Christians were to explore ways of thinking about that day, their preachers needed, surely, to step up to the mark.

When I was asked to preach on the first Sunday of 2019, the year in which Britain seemed to face much turmoil, I was convinced that any preacher that day needed to somehow set a tone for the year ahead. I was also convinced that sermons should be political, but not party political, and that unity not uniformity is the call of the Church. The sermon for Epiphany is given below.

Sermon 7: Epiphany 2019

Once upon a time there were some very wise people, people of great learning, who vaguely wondered what the coming year might bring. All the great literature of the time, and all the religions of the world suggested that there was someone greater than themselves. A king the like of which no one had ever seen. And something in them yearned to see a new age dawn. Suddenly, one night as they gathered for study, a bright light shone out. It was so bright they couldn't tell whether it was in the sky or in their own spirits, but they did know that it was calling them, and that its tug on their heartstrings was what they had been yearning for all their lives.

The rest is in today's Gospel reading. These wise people – they were not kings, there were probably more than three, and it is more than possible that women were among them – these wise people made a difference. News of the commonwealth of God spread out from the people of Israel to Gentiles – you and me, partly through these foreigners from the East.

The way their story has been told down the centuries, they have been made special – because of power, or wealth, or influence. They have become a small number – three; and they have been made kings – powerful men. Yet none of those are reasons why Matthew mentions them in his Gospel. Matthew introduces them by mentioning two actions – they observed, and they came to worship.

Observing has something to do with our orientation. Apparently the Jewish leaders of the time knew of the same prophecies as the Magi, and they must have seen the same star. The difference is that they didn't notice it, didn't connect what they knew with what they saw. I suspect that their understanding of the ancient prophecies engendered in them a yearning that led to them noticing the star. Maybe that's the reason why in our country at the moment, amid the mistrust and uncertainty, church attendance is once again rising, and the number of atheists is falling. There is a yearning for something bigger, something beyond ourselves and our petty quarrels. Observation is key to growing the commonwealth of God. How many Old Testament stories depend on someone first observing? Moses noticed the burning bush; Daniel observed the culture of Babylon. If I am going to see God at work, and God always *is* at work, I have to adopt an attitude akin to that of C. S. Lewis, who said: 'I believe in Christianity as I believe that the sun has risen: not because I see it, but because by it I see everything else.'

Seeing is not enough, of course. The Magi see and then they act – 'we have come'. They were wise people, acknowledged as such, I assume. They could have observed, and then sat back and talked about their insightful understanding. Perhaps, as news of Jesus spread, later in his life, they could have said, 'Ah, yes, we saw that coming.'

Perhaps there's a warning for you and me here. With long experience and a great deal of study perhaps we might easily be lulled into thinking we've got the answers. Yet like the star, God moves on ahead of us. And God expects us to move too, to continue to follow. When they arrive in Jerusalem they state simply why they are there – to worship the new king. Perhaps they had taken their eye off the star for a while, as they approached the moment of revelation. Certainly they seem to assume the new ruler will be born at the seat of power, nearer to Herod's throne than to a woman's lap. The ancient wisdom of the Hebrew Bible, our Old Testament, interpreted by Herod's advisers, points them in the right direction once again.

And what do they find? Leaving alone the stories that have grown up around this scene, and the carol that seems to place these people at the manger, the evidence we have suggests Jesus was a toddler by this point. These folk from the East arrive not at the cotside of a newborn, but in the home of a toddler. Thinking about this as we spent time with our 18-month-old grandson over Christmas, I wondered whether the early Church that was accused of turning the world upside down was simply emulating the example of the toddler Christ. I wonder what happened on this visit. Perhaps Jesus the toddler climbed on the box of frankincense to get something down off the shelf.

No matter. God was discovered in the ordinary, with his mother at home.

Seeing leads to moving for these wise seekers of Jesus. It must do for us too.

And moving is costly. The group leave home, they travel to a strange land, they bring expensive gifts. They show commitment. They persevere. Commitment needs perseverance to achieve anything.

Every January fitness companies and diet companies and gyms take vast sums of money from people who determine that this year they will lose weight, or get fit. By the end of the month most of those people have stopped attending classes, and in 12 months' time the majority will weigh just the same, and be exactly as fit as they are now.

Observation – I'm overweight; movement – I'll register with a gym; commitment – I'll pay the fee – all need perseverance, if they are to amount to anything. It's how things change. I know, for example, that single-use plastic is damaging the world that I live in and that my grandchildren will inherit. I have decided that I will avoid supermarket carrier bags. And yet, I forget to take alternatives with me too often.

I wonder what the Magi told people when they got back home? How do you explain the yearning in your heart that persuades you to embark on a journey to who knows where? How do you tell people that your commitment and expense led to an ordinary home? How do you explain that there, not in a palace, was where you worshipped God?

Maybe they doubted what they had seen. Maybe people couldn't or, like Herod, wouldn't accept it. Could they make anyone believe? No. All they could do, after their yearning and travelling and worshipping, was to say, 'This is how it was. This is what we have seen. Make of it what you will.'

So what does Epiphany and today's Scripture say to us?

This is how I see it – make of it what you will.

Today is the first Sunday of what seems likely to be one of the most turbulent years in our nation's recent history. We are being forced to decide what kind of a nation we want to be, and perhaps missing what kind of nation we are already becoming. A major incident has been declared, resulting in the deployment of resources and funds. It is not the 3,700 families forced to visit a food bank on an average day; or the 5,400 victims of daily domestic violence; or even the 4,750 people forced to sleep rough on our streets every night. It is the handful of asylum seekers who risk their lives to get here because their lives are at risk back home. Whatever the rights and wrongs of the case, the response shows us what kind of a nation we are in danger of becoming. I don't think our parliament is known for reasoned debate anyway, but it is becoming more polarized and venomous. That does not reflect only on our MPs. It's how debate in the local community is going too. We are not disagreeing well. Archbishop Justin has repeatedly over the last two years encouraged us, as the body of Christ, to model good disagreement.

Our call this year, perhaps more than ever, comes from the start of today's Old Testament reading, Isaiah 60.1: 'Arise, shine, for your light has come and the glory of the Lord has risen upon you.' We have to observe the times. We must be ready to come and worship. And we must never tire of looking at things in the light of our faith. As a start, that may not mean agreeing about everything. But it certainly does mean that when we disagree we need to do it well. And that might mean bold conversation, and courageous Bible study. After all, all it takes for evil to triumph is for good people to do nothing.

Time for reflection

Models are not really instructions or prescriptions. Rather they reflect what happens, or might happen. *Do you have a conscious model of preaching?*

In some circles it seems fashionable to denigrate the sermon. David Norrington (1996) claimed it has no New Testament basis, and Jonnie Baker claimed, 'a talking head is actually a very ineffective means of communication. People retain only a very small percentage of information communicated in this way' (2009: 14). It will be clear from what I have said that I have a high view of preaching. It is a unique means by which we can explore faith in a scripturally rooted way, wrestling with difficulties honestly, and dealing with issues sincerely. People tend to invest time in what they value. *What does the amount of time you allocate to preaching say about the value you place on it?*

Daring to be a woman preacher

Lord, dare I preach?
With what wisdom do I open my mouth?
What kind teaching is on my tongue?

Can I magnify my Lord?
Speak comfort to the lowly?
Offer food to the hungry?
Can I sing of the Lord's triumph?

Speak out to kings and rulers?
Whisper justice in the ears of the powerful?

'Take heart, daughter, your faith makes you whole.'
'Go tell his disciples he is alive.'
'You are favoured.'

Spend time reflecting on this poem, and allowing God to speak to you.

Notes

1 Alfie Evans (9 May 2016–28 April 2018) was a baby boy from Liverpool born with a terminal condition. The medical team and his parents disagreed about his end-of-life care, which resulted in a legal battle and online abuse for both sides.

2 The Wisdom Commentary project is redressing the balance. It is the first scholarly collaboration to offer detailed feminist interpretation of every book of the Bible.

8

Preaching Women

In this book I have explored 'the different perspectives and enriching possibilities that women bring to the preaching of God's word' (Copeland, 2014: 26). Preparing to preach begins with who we are and what we have seen. The moment of a sermon's beginning is almost impossible to pin down, for preachers are always gathering ideas and experiences. Living life as a preacher is rather like beachcombing. Our senses are finely tuned to spot moments pregnant with meaning, objects that speak of God, times that immerse us in the transcendent or bring us crashing to earth with a new understanding of creation or humanity. As we collect all of these treasures, our preacher's rucksack becomes a store chest of images and ideas and impressions that link us with our hearers and our God in ways that make our preaching live. While all preachers should do this, it is being a woman that makes the contents of our rucksack different from our male colleagues. We experience the world as women. Our bodies, through the regular cycles they go through, teach us things men's bodies can never know. It is both informative and humbling to read the stories of people who were once one gender and are now another. Rachel Mann, a transwoman Anglican priest, wrote that 'To become a woman was a step away from power and status.'[1] Thomas Page McBee, whose book *Amateur* was a Radio 4 book of the week, explored the experience of learning to become aggressive, having been raised as a passive female. It is we who are judged for inhabiting a female body. It is we who are able to identify most closely with women who are oppressed for being women. It is we who are touched inappropriately, spoken to suggestively or dismissed arrogantly. Each experience gives us unique things to say. Where we live forms the outer circle of my model. It is where we derive our experience and form our positions; where we are shaped by tradition and culture. The second circle is where we work with our gathered treasures, shaping them by reflection, gaining insight from them and working out how to communicate them. At the centre of all this lies the sermon.

I have sometimes thought that each of us really has only one sermon. It is a long sermon, of course, too long to be given in one go, certainly, perhaps too long to ever be given in full even over the period of a lifetime, but one cohesive sermon nonetheless. From it we choose elements that construct what we say at any one time. As we live and work and reflect, the overall sermon changes, or its emphases develop. It is worth spending time with this sermon, reflecting deeply on what it is that makes me 'me', and how that affects what I might say from the pulpit.

Fundamental to this work is truth telling. Telling the truth about ourselves, our churches, our Bible and our culture: calling out sexism and patriarchy for their oppression not just of other women, but of 'me too'; searching relentlessly for Bible women who can provide role models to follow, or expressions of what is wrong in their, and our, culture; exploring women's experiences of God and faith and sin, so that we can speak honestly to others. Right and true outcomes of preaching are as different as the places where God's word is entered into, and the communities in which it is heard. When these outcomes are based on real experience they can highlight positive differ-ence as integral to the gospel message of hope. Or, they can challenge negative difference with the gospel of justice. The differences women preachers celebrate need not polarize, but have power instead to draw attention to the rich diversity of God's creation. Exercising women's preaching gifts has pro-phetic potential to portray the wholeness of God's image in each of us, and in the body of Christ, the Church.

The Bible and doctrine alone might inform what preachers

say about God, but they can only ever lead to univocal proclamation which is alienating, particularly for women. Developing women's preaching, and women preachers, is not simply about equality. It is much more important than that. It drives at the heart of God's self-revelation to and through humanity, and God's performative grace in creation. When God's revelation is warped by exclusion, or dismembered by suppression, all people suffer. The fullness of God's presence in our lives needs God's activity in both women and men to be manifest, otherwise both excluded women and exalted men suffer.

Change never comes from the centre. Those in power have too much to lose. Change comes from the margins and is brought about by those who dare. My prayer is that this book will inspire and encourage women preachers to speak as women and for women each time they preach, so that the fullness of God's nature might be seen among us.

Note

1 'I'm a woman, but I'm glad I used to be a man', 9 June 2014, on Transformation: where love meets social justice website.

Bibliography

Aries, E. (1996). *Men and Women in Interaction*. Oxford: Oxford University Press.

Auden, W. (1994). *Tell Me the Truth about Love: Ten Poems*. New York: Vintage.

Baker, J. (2009). *Transforming Preaching: Communicating God's Word in a Postmodern World*. Cambridge: Grove Publishing Ltd.

Bates, L. *Everyday Sexism*. London: Simon and Schuster UK Ltd.

Beckett, L. (16 March 2019). 'White Men are Considered Everyone': Ocasio-Cortez calls out poll stories bias. *The Guardian*.

Bennett, Z. (2002). *Introducing Feminist Perspectives on Pastoral Theology*. London: Sheffield Academic Press.

Biddulph, S. (2008). *Raising Boys: Why Boys are Different – and How to Help Them Become Happy and Well-Balanced Men*. London: Thorsons.

Bird, M. (2016). *Romans (The Story of God Bible Commentary)*. Grand Rapids, MI: Zondervan.

Bowie, F. and Davies, O. (eds) (1990). *Hildegard of Bingen: Mystical Writings*. New York: Crossroad.

Brown, R. (1999). *The Birth of the Messiah: A Commentary on the Infancy Narratives in the Gospels of Matthew and Luke*. New Haven and London: The Anchor Yale Bible.

Brown Taylor, B. (2014). *Learning to Walk in the Dark: Because God Often Shows Up at Night*. Norwich: Canterbury Press (Kindle edn).

Brueggemann, W. (1997). *Cadences of Home: Preaching Among Exiles*. Louisville, KY: John Knox Press.

Brueggemann, W. (2010). *The Word Militant: Preaching a Decentering Word*. Minneapolis, MN: Fortress Press.

Bultmann, R. (1965). Is Exegesis without Presuppositions Possible? In Ogden, S. (ed.), *Existence and Faith: Shorter Writings of Rudolph Bultmann*. London: Hodder & Stoughton.

Buttrick, D. (1987). *Homiletic Moves and Structures*. Philadelphia, PA: Fortress Press.

Carlyle, T. (1841). *On Heroes, Hero-Worship, and the Heroic in History*. London: James Fraser.

Chodorow, N. (1978). *The Reproduction of Mothering: Psychoanalysis and the Sociology of Gender*. Berkeley: University of California Press.

Chopp, R. (1995). *Saving Work: Feminist Practices of Theological Education*. Louisville, KY: John Knox Press.

Chopp, R. (2002). *The Power to Speak: Feminism, Language, God*. Eugene, OR: Wipf and Stock.

Churches Together in Britain and Ireland (2001). *Mary Magdalene: Apostle to the Apostles*. London: Churches Together.

Copeland, J. (2014). *Feminine Registers: The Importance of Women's Voices for Christian Preaching*. Eugene, OR: Cascade Books.

Craddock, F. (1985). *As One without Authority*. Nashville, TN: Abingdon.

Criado Perez, C. (2019). *Invisible Women: Exposing Data Bias in a World Designed for Men*. London: Chatto & Windus.

De Beauvoir, S. (1949, 2010). *The Second Sex*. Trans. Borde, C. and Malovaney-Chavllier, S. London: Vintage Books.

Durber, S. (2007). *Preaching Like a Woman*. London: SPCK.

Fowler, J. (1981). *Stages of Faith: The Psychology of Human Development and the Quest for Meaning*. New York: HarperOne.

Freeman, L. (2014). *Bible Women: All Their Words and Why They Matter*. Cincinnati, OH: Forward Movement Publications (Kindle edn 391).

Frei, H. (1974). *The Eclipse of Biblical Narrative*. New Haven, CT: Yale University Press.

Gilligan, C. (1982). *In a Different Voice: Psychological Theory and Women's Development*. Cambridge, MA: Harvard University Press.

Glick, P. and Fiske, S. (2001). An Ambivalent Alliance: Hostile and Benevolent Sexism as Complementary Justifications for Gender Inequality. *American Psychologist*, pp. 109–18.

Goffman, E. (1990). *The Presentation of Self in Everyday Life*. London: Penguin.

Goodbourn, D. (1996). Overcoming Barriers to Adult Christian Education. *Ministry Today*.

Graham, E. (2014). Feminist Theory. In Miller-McLemore, B. S. (ed.), *The Wiley Blackwell Companion to Practical Theology*. Chichester: John Wiley and Sons Ltd.

Gross, N. L. (2017). *Women's Voices and the Practice of Preaching*. Grand Rapids, MI: Eerdmans.

Guenther, M. (1992). *Holy Listening: The Art of Spiritual Direction*. London: Darton, Longman and Todd.

Guinness, M. (2003). *Woman: The Full Story – A Dynamic Celebration of Freedoms*. Grand Rapids, MI: Zondervan.

Gutiérrez, G. (1999). The Task and Content of Liberation Theology. In Rowland, C. (ed.), *The Cambridge Companion to Liberation Theology*. Cambridge: Cambridge University Press (pp. 25–32).

Hardin Freeman, L. (2014). *Bible Women: All Their Words and Why They Matter*. Forward Movement Publications (Kindle edn).

Henry, Matthew. https://biblehub.com/commentaries/mhcw/acts.16.htm

Hull, J. (2011). *What Prevents Christian Adults from Learning?* London: SCM Press.

Irenaeus. (1952). *Proof of the Apostolic Preaching*. Trans Smith, J. London: Longmans, Green and Co.

Joung, E. (2013). Patterns of Women's Religious Attachments. In Slee, N., Porter, F. and Phillips, A. (eds), *The Faith Lives of Women and Girls*. London and New York: Routledge (pp. 161–71).

Jung, C. (1921). *Psychological Types*. www.jungiananalysts.org.uk/wp-content/uploads/2018/07/C.-G.-Jung-Collected-Works-Volume-6-Psychological-Types.pdf

Keener, C. (1993). *The IVP Bible Background Commentary: New Testament*. Downers Grove, IL: InterVarsity Press.

King, K. (1998). Prophetic Power and Women's Authority: The Case of the Gospel of Mary (Magdalene). In Mayne Kienzle, B. and Walker, P. (eds), *Women Preachers and Prophets through Two Millennia of Christianity*. Berkeley, CA: University of Berkeley Press (pp. 21–41).

Kohlberg, L. (1981). *The Philosophy of Moral Development*. New York: Harper and Row.

Lammers Gross, N. (2017). *Women's Voices and the Practice of Preaching*. Grand Rapids, MI: Eerdmans.

Lawless, E. (2015). *Women Preaching Revolution: Calling for Connection in a Disconnected Time*. Philadelphia, PA: University of Philadelphia.

Lewis, K. (2016). *SHE: Five Keys to Unlock the Power of Women in Ministry*. Nashville, TN: Abingdon.

Llewellyn, D. (2015). *Reading, Feminism and Spirituality: Troubling the Waves*. London: Palgrave MacMillan.

Long, T. (1988). *The Senses of Preaching*. Atlanta, GA: Westminster John Knox Press.

Lyotard, J. (1979). The Postmodern Condition: A Report on Knowledge. *Theory and History of Literature*, 10.

Mann, R. (2010). Presiding from the Broken Middle. In Slee, N. and Burns, S. (eds), *Presiding Like a Woman: Feminist Gestures for Christian Assemblies*. London: SPCK.

McDaid, H. and Jones, L. (2017). *Nasty Women: A Collection of Essays and Accounts on What it is to be a Woman in the 21st Century*. 404 Ink.

Miller, J. B. (1986 [1976]). *Toward a New Psychology of Women*. Boston, MA: Beacon Press.

Moltmann-Wendel, E. (1982). *The Women Around Jesus*. London: SCM Press.

Morton, N. (1985). *The Journey is Home*. Boston, NY: Beacon Press.

Murphy-O'Connor, J. (2008). *The Holy Land: An Oxford Archae-ological Guide (Oxford Archaeological Guides): An Oxford Archaeological Guide from Earliest times to 1700.* Oxford: Oxford University Press.

Murray, J. (2017). *A History of Britain in 21 Women.* London: Oneworld Publications.

Murray, J. (2018). *A History of the World in 21 Women.* London: Oneworld Publications.

Norrington, D. (1996). *To Preach or Not to Preach: The Church's Urgent Question.* Carlisle: Paternoster Press.

O'Murchu, D. (2015). *Inclusivity: A Gospel Mandate.* Maryknoll, NY: Orbis Books.

Oneill, T. (2013). 7 tips for keeping your man (from the 1950s). *The Week*, 14 August.

Page McBee, T. (2019). *Amateur: A Reckoning with Gender, Identity and Masculinity.* Edinburgh: Canongate Books. www.bbc.co.uk/programmes/po6tmdqv

Peck, M. S. (1987). *The Different Drum.* London: Random House.

Piaget, J. (1929). *A Child's Concept of the World.* New York: Harcourt, Brace and Company.

Piaget J. (1962). *Play, Dreams and Imitation in Childhood.* New York: WW Norton.

Podles, L. (1999). *The Church Impotent: The Feminization of Christianity.* Dallas, TX: Spence Pub.

Purvis-Smith, V. (2005). Gender and the Aesthetic of Preaching. In Day, D., Astley, J. and Francis, L. (eds), *A Reader on Preaching: Making Connections.* Farnham: Ashgate.

Radford Ruether, R. (1983). *Sexism and God-Talk: Toward a Feminist Theology.* London: SCM Press.

Ricoeur, P. (1977). *Freud and Philosophy: An Essay on Interpretation (The Terry Lectures Series).* New Haven, CT: Yale University Press.

Ricoeur, P. (1980). The Hermeneutics of Testimony. In Mudge, L. (ed.), *Essays on Biblical Interpretation.* Philadelphia, PA: Fortress Press.

Riesbeck, D. (2015). Aristotle on the Politics of Marriage: 'Marital Rule' in the Politis. *The Classical Quarterly*, Vol. 65, Issue 1, May, pp. 134–52.

Romanes, G. (1887). Mental Differences of Men and Women. *Popular Science Monthly*, July.

Saini, A. (2018). *Inferior: The True Power of Women and the Science that Shows It.* London: 4th Estate.

Saiving, V. G. (1960). The Human Situation: A Feminine View. *Journal of Religion*, 40.2, pp. 100–12.

Schleiermacher, F. (1806). *Christmas Eve: Dialogue on the Incarnation.* Eugene, OR: Cascade Books.

Schüssler-Fiorenza, E. (1994). *In Memory of Her: A Feminist Theological Reconstruction of Christian Origins*. The Crossroad Company.

Slee, N. (2004). *Praying Like a Woman*. London: SPCK.

Spivak, G. (1994). Can the Subaltern Speak? In Williams, P. and Chrisman, L. (eds), *Colonial Discourse and Post-colonial Theory: A Reader*. Hertfordshire: Harvester Wheatsheaf.

Storkey, E. (1989). *What's Right with Feminism?* London: SPCK.

Storkey, E. (2015). *Scars Across Humanity: Understanding and Overcoming Violence against Women*. London: SPCK.

Strhan, A. (2015). *Aliens and Strangers: The Struggle for Coherence in the Everyday Lives of Evangelicals*. Oxford: Oxford University Press.

Sweet, L. (2014). *Giving Blood: A Fresh Paradigm for Preaching*. Grand Rapids, MI: Zondervan.

Trible, P. (1984). *Texts of Terror: Literary-Feminist Readings of Biblical Narratives*. Philadelphia, PA: Fortress Press.

Tryer, A. (1951). *Sex, Satisfaction and Happy Marriage*. Emerson Books Inc.

Walton, H. and Durber, S. (1994). *Silence in Heaven: A Book of Women's Preaching*. London: SCM Press.

Wellard, S. (2011). *Doing it All? Grandparents, Childcare and Employment: An Analysis of British Social Attitudes Survey Data from 1998 and 2009*. Grandparents Plus.

Williams, J. (2014). *God Remembered Rachel: Women's Stories in the Old Testament and Why They Matter*. London: SPCK.

Wink, W. (1973). *The Bible in Human Transformation*. Minneapolis, MN: Fortress Press.

Wright, N. (2013). *Paul and the Faithfulness of God*. London: SPCK.

Wuthnow, R. (1994). *Sharing the Journey: Support Groups and America's New Quest for Community*. New York: Simon and Schuster.

Index of Names and Subjects